The Prison Notes

584

ISBN: 978-91-87339-24-0

THE
PRISON
NOTES

CORNELIU ZELEA CODREANU

LOGIK FÖRLAG

Corneliu Zelea Codreanu

TABLE OF CONTENTS

INTRODUCTION

The following Introduction was written by Faust Bradesco, a Romanian Legionary veteran and intellectual who continued defending Codreanu's legacy in several books after being exiled to France following the Communist occupation of his homeland, and where he was to spend the remainder of his life. This Introduction was originally published in the French edition of the Prison Notes *in 1986.*

This short work, already translated into several languages, now brings to completion in French the knowledge and understanding of the tragic life of Corneliu Zelea Codreanu, the legendary leader of the Romanian Legionary Movement, otherwise known as the Iron Guard.

It is concerned with a very short period of time – 19 April to 19 June 1938 – during which he was incarcerated in the prison of Jilava in the most vile and discouraging conditions. A mere two months, but months which transformed the fine, proud hero into a Christian martyr.

His thoughts and his behaviour during this short time do not evoke a doctrinal attempt to explain the Legionary phenomenon, or even to deepen that which made up his political thought. Rather there is an attempt to put into practice the core of a doctrine which tears the individual away from the domination of matter, so as to bring him to spiritual fulfillment.

These brief notes, sometimes sketchy, marked by brief allusions to his private life and to his family, by details regarding his health and his morale, seem to record some facts which ought to have been developed someday at leisure. It was not possible for him to do otherwise: the escape from prison of these small pieces of paper, written in haste in truncated sentences, sometimes badly written, is already miraculous.

In order to understand fully the meaning and importance of this short work, two phases must be identified.

1. *The despair of the hunted man,* who feels the hatred all around him and suffers a moral torture.

During this first phase, there is no depth to the text: just short notes and repetitions. One has the distinct impression that it is a question of points to be returned to at a later time, of the milestones of a suffering man who hopes to regain his freedom. Such is his state of mind until his shameful and unjust condemnation.

2. Then, *the bursting forth of Christian enlightenment,* when his soul finally realises the importance of the spiritual change of the individual through the approach to and communion with the Godhead.

This is the phase where his inner transformation is effected, when he grasps fully the greatness of the divine presence in the life of man and society. The sentences are more detailed, as if he felt that he would never have the time to look at them again and to blend them into a maturely considered and structured whole.

It urges on his death; he says so. But, as time passes, and as his thoughts bring him towards a metaphysical and spiritual understanding of human perfection, he is overwhelmed by peace, brought on not by mere wisdom, but by the purely theological.

The spiritual sense of life – social, political, or quite simply human – advocated by Legionary doctrine, is no longer a potentiality, something to be brought into being. It is an actual fact, and of its nature holy. The three theological virtues, Faith, Hope and Charity, which also make up the essence of Legionary doctrine, opens up to the 'New Man' (understood and put into relief by the Iron Guard) the path of *moral perfection, right reason* and *spiritual improvement.*

***

The two months of prison described in this work represent a period, *not new* but *different,* from so many others that the leader of the Iron Guard underwent behind bars. Different, not so much because of the moral agonies or the physical tortures, but above all because of the spiritual transformation which shows itself in him. Interiorly he suffers a torment which affects him in his depths, because it is doubly distressing:

a) *Physically*: he is ill, suffering greatly which brings on fever; he is extremely emotional, given over to despair and to pessimism.

b) *Morally*: he is exhausted by so many battles and victories, reduced to ash by the hatred which is hunting him down. He is repelled and indignant at the injustice which overwhelms him and reduces him to a mere chained inmate.

He is on the point of collapse, at the difficult moment of struggle between *the massive weight of calumnies and lies,* heaped upon his weakened shoulders, and his *moral conscience,* sustained by his indomitable but chained will. Every effort at every moment seems like a merciless clash between Good and Evil, between the devouring forces of Darkness and the unending glory of heavenly light.

Reduced to the vegetative state of the condemned man by the good offices of the hidden forces which rule the world, he, the man of granite, of vision, of free will, suffers the calvary of powerlessness and doubt. And this, as much for himself as for his family, for the Legionaries and for his country. Spiritual confusion weighs ever more heavily upon the society which he wants to save, and to which he has vouchsafed his life. His thought falters under the weight of despair. His distress brings him to the pitch of discouragement which is crushing him.

Feeling himself about to collapse, he reacts. He must regain the upper hand. His duty imposes itself upon his state of mind. His soul responds, and the cogwheels of his deep faith take on their rhythm once again. He hurls himself into the understanding of religious truth, which fills him with an ineffable bliss. Through prayer and meditation, he plumbs the Christian mystery. His faith strengthens him. His spirit takes on other dimensions, which propel him above and beyond ordinary life.

In this inner reconstruction takes place the unseen spiritual transformation of Corneliu Codreanu, and it is in this that is to be found the importance of this work, which appears at first sight to be unremarkable. In the life of this exceptional man, a life during which *action and faith* have moulded the pillars of his existential reality, an unexpected and transcendent point opens to him an understanding of divine oneness. Through reading the *Gospels,* in the spiritual state which was imparted to him by his arbitrary status as prisoner, he grasped the true depth of the presence of God.

The parallels that he makes between his calvary and that of Jesus Christ are hardly thoughts born of pride, but simply the dazzling understanding of the way which leads to redemption and fulfillment. He throws himself into it, fully aware of the good that this represents for the individual in himself and for society which, one day, is going to perceive the meaning. He considers his accomplishment in religious truth as a merit badge given to the cause of the Legionary Movement, whose objective is precisely the raising of the individual above contingencies and the human condition, an upward surging towards the supreme truth.

Thus, the few pages of this work show – in their painful forward movement, full of moral suffering, despair, doubts and bewildered questionings – the change of a soul which always believed and which, in the end, found the divine meaning of human worth and existence.

The whole philosophy of sacrifice, of suffering and of love, with which he had furnished his movement, received thereby a priceless meaning and scope. Thus, the *personal perfection* which each must seek, the *respect for others* that each must adopt, the *fulfillment of duty* that each must undertake, appears as an ideal to be achieved through the application of the virtues which make us in the image of God. The efforts, the sacrifices of love become the path of understanding of the Biblical message and of improvement.

***

In reading these *Notes*, one must not expect some kind of *political testament*, full of philosophical thoughts or of practical advice for the future. Neither is it a politico-literary essay of the sort represented by *Memories of Prison* or *My Days with the Outlaws*. It is something altogether different, which is really important for every individual, whosoever he might be.

In these two months of tribulations, Corneliu Zelea Codreanu discovers, at the same time as the sad barbarism of our century governed by pitiless forces, the regal gates of human rebirth. He lives an experience which must remain an ideal model for all members of the Iron Guard.

And, if there is a message to be taken from these pathetic lines, we find it in these two phrases:

– Mankind needs 'a school for great improvement and profound Christian morality'.

– 'Pain upon pain, suffering upon suffering, agony upon agony, wound upon wound in our bodies and in our souls, and fall after fall: thus shall we conquer.'

FAUST BRADESCO

The Foreword presented here was written for the original edition of The Prison Notes (or Notes from Jilava, *the title under which it was first printed) by Horia Sima in June 1951. He was the immediate successor to Codreanu in leading the Legionary Movement, and was to remain so until his death in Spain in 1993.*

Although he faced an almost impossible task in replacing the Captain in the aftermath of a terrible and bloody repression by King Carol, he managed to bring order from chaos and to help form the government of the National Legionary State during the Second World War. From the outset, he refused the title Captain, saying that it could only ever apply to one man in the history of the Romanian Legionary movement, with the result that he became simply the Commander of the Legion.

Throughout his years in exile, he, like so many Legionaries, was intensely active in keeping the Legion alive, and strove to make a new and younger generation aware of the truth of the Legionary phenomenon. He wrote a great many books and articles during his long life, but most of them have never appeared in the English language.

FOREWORD

Thirteen years after the martyrdom of the Captain at Jilava, we are publishing his notes of the time when he was locked up in prison. They were published for the first time in Rostock, Germany, in the form of a crude pamphlet. It was impossible for us to have them printed properly at that time. The German government had made an agreement with Antonescu to keep us in concentration camps, and also to censor any Legionary appearance in the European press. A Dutch-language edition of Corneliu Codreanu's book, *For My Legionaries*, was banned and the edition prepared in French suffered the same fate. It is only in Spain that the Captain's book received a different reception.The Europe which pretended to be nationalist barred every possible avenue of expression to us and, by a paradox of history, it is only today that we can assert our ideas freely.

Notes from Jilava is a pathetic human document. They recount the witness of a man who knows that he can no longer expect anything from other men, and that for his life and his struggle, which began from the moment the King put himself at the head of the clique of evildoers, he places himself in the hands of God. His physical and moral suffering is confided to posterity, as he knows that his death is imminent. Those who follow the Captain's stations of the Cross can empathise as he is tested by doubt, sadness, and despair, as they assault his generous soul.

Then, suddenly, in the darkness of Jilava, the light of another world flickers. The distant past comes to his aid when Christ carries His Cross to the place of his condemnation. The Captain is no longer alone. The Truth witnesses for him. And the Truth will triumph over all the efforts of those who sentenced him to death. 'God sees and will reward': such are the words with which he completes his last entry, given to other judges than those who condemned him.

These notes are also important from another point of view. *Notes from Jilava* makes clear, in a manner which leaves no doubt, the deep meaning of Legionary wisdom: the spiritual cannot be disconnected from politics; the interior attitudes of the individual, his supernatural desires, must find expression in the aspirations of communal life. 'The mark of our time', said Codreanu, 'is that we are above all concerned with the struggle between ourselves and other men, and barely at all with the struggle between the commandments of the Holy Ghost and the desires of our earthly nature. The Legionary Movement is an exception in concerning itself also, however insufficiently, with the Christian victory in man for his salvation.'

'The responsibility of a leader is very great. He must not flatter his troops with earthly victories, without preparing them at the same time for the decisive struggle, from which the soul of each person can emerge, crowned with an eternal victory or a total defeat.'

The whole tragedy of mankind stems from the dislocation of these two elements, from the false conception of a history that exists without God, under the pretext that social laws should be different from those which govern the inner man.

HORIA SIMA

TUESDAY, 19 APRIL 1938

It is nine o'clock in the evening. Led by a police captain and an adjutant, I go down the stairs of the Department of War.

Outside, the Black Maria.[1] Every time I see it, my soul is embittered.

The door opens and I go in. Inside, total darkness. I can barely make out the outlines of four soldiers. 'Load weapons', I hear the adjutant command. We leave. We are passing through illuminated streets. At a certain moment, I realise that we are on the Izvor Bridge, not far from the General's[2] house, where, until a few days earlier, our national headquarters was located. And we will return to it, with the help of God.

We take a left turn, then drive along the quay of Damovitza. I am being taken to Vacaresti, I tell myself. And the roads disappear, one after the other.

Then, I sense that we have left Bucharest. I no longer hear the noise of cars, buses and trams and I no longer see light through the slits in the roof.

The Black Maria speeds along the road toward the unknown.

After a while, it is stopped by a group of guards. 'Stop! Who goes there?'

---

1   A type of vehicle used to transport prisoners.

2   General Gheorghe Cantacuzino-Grănicerul (1869-1937) was a hero of the First World War who later became a prominent supporter of Codreanu. Codreanu briefly turned leadership of the Iron Guard over to him when he was forced into hiding following the killing of Duca in 1933. He was also one of the co-founders of Codreanu's All for the Fatherland Party in 1935, and went to Spain in support of the Guard's fighting on behalf of the nationalists in the Civil War. These activities were praised by the young Mircea Eliade, among others.

15

Ion Mota and Sterie Ciumeti in Jilava prison, Christmas 1933.

Vasile Marin and Sterie Ciumeti in Jilava prison.

'Let us through, it's the police.' A little further, another roadblock. Finally, we stop. I am let out at Jilava, in front of the administration office. Jilava is an old fort of the Bucharest belt, built in the reign of King Carol I, after the war of 1877. Now, it is a military prison.

It is here that Mota, Marin, Ciumeti, the General and hundreds of comrades suffered in 1933-34.[3]

We enter the administration office. After a little while, the Prison Governor and two officers of the guard arrive.

While I am there, they receive orders by telephone.

The police captain and the adjutant who have brought me here regretfully take their leave of me. Two chosen souls, who are an exception in this force.

The Governor asks me to give him my tie. Then, the money: 1,000 lei. My pockets are searched. Horrible! But it is the rulebook which demands it. I leave with Lieutenant Mastacan, flanked by four guards, with bayonets fixed.

I am tired.

We go into the fort. We walk along vaulted corridors, which are long and painful and completely dark. A dank smell, cold and moist, hits me.

Then I am put into a room about seven metres long and five wide.

From one side to the other, wooden planks, resting upon trestles also made of wood, make up two big, communal beds. A barred window looks out onto one of the walls of the fort, about ten metres high. Above this room, there is almost five metres of earth. The outer walls are about two metres thick. The floor is made of asphalt.

If, outside, I had seen a man wishing to sleep even for half an hour in such a place, I would have stopped him and said, 'Do not, you will hurt yourself.'

The adjutant brings me a straw mattress and two large blankets. He puts them on the planks. He gives me nothing on which to rest my head.

The lieutenant knows that all this lacks even the most basic decency. He feels uneasy and excuses himself by saying that the rules demand it. He asks me if I have a cap because I will be very cold during the night. Where could I have got one?

He utters a few more kind words and then leaves, bolting the door. From head to foot, the big walls everywhere pierce my body with frozen arrows of dampness. One could say that these strange walls,

---

3   On 10 December 1933, Liberal Prime Minister Ion Duca banned Codreanu's Iron Guard, killing and imprisoning many of its members. The Legionaries responded by assassinating Duca on 29 December 1933.

within which one recognises nothing of oneself and in which one sees nothing of one's family, these hostile walls are only waiting for a human life so as to destroy it by sending thousands of arrows, like real shafts of death, into the body of the miserable, condemned man. I sleep. A long night.

HOLY EASTER, 24 APRIL 1938

Dampness is entering my bones.

I am breathing the air of this cellar. I can feel my lungs pierced by needles, by bullets.

I am stretched out on the bed of planks. My bones hurt. I remain five minutes on one side, five minutes on the other.

I turn onto my left side. I hear my heart beating. Or perhaps it is drops of blood which are falling?

Life is flowing out of the exhausted body.

O Country! How you reward your sons!

I fell asleep. I dreamt of Mum and Elvira Garneata. Elvira allows me to drink from a large jug of water. Mum tells me, 'Life was too painful. We've moved from here.' (It was in a village in the suburb of Husi, near the River Prut.)

I say to her, 'I am going to the top of the hill with Nicoleta and Horodniceanu and, when I return, I will leave you a little money. Don't worry.'

And I left. It was nighttime. A full, bright Moon lit up the Earth.

***

I am afraid that something will happen to her. My mother is alone once again! A son-in-law dead in Spain, a widowed daughter with two children. Me, in prison. Four other children, also in prison or about to be arrested. One amongst these also has four children without anything to eat.

My father, gone to Bucharest to pick up his pension before the holidays, never returned. He was arrested and taken to an unknown place.

Nobody knows his fate.

At home, mother is waiting for us to celebrate Easter with her. The joys of an old mother are so few; she can rarely get all of her children together at once!

Ion Mota and Vasile Marin.

*General Cantacuzino-
Grănicerul. He led the
contingent of Legionaries
who fought in the Spanish
Civil War.*

*The coffins of Ion Mota and Vasile Marin carried in procession to the cathe-
dral in Cernauti, accompanied by a group of German students.*

At our home, at Easter, it is a desert. None of those awaited are present. Not one soul comes near my mother. All the neighbours avoid her and, out of fear, do not even approach the house.

A heart beats, alone, and seeks after us in the prisons, running from cell to cell to find us, to comfort us, to embrace our suffering bodies.

But what to do, when no one tells you anything and when you receive no news?

O mother, who cries alone in a corner of the house and who no one sees, know that we, too, cry for you, on this Easter day, each of us in our cell!

***

Yesterday, Saturday, I asked that the barber come to cut my beard, which had grown bushy after a week on my frozen face. The prison barber, a poor, condemned gypsy, came. He shaved me and, for the first time in a week, I washed my face.

I am awaiting the Resurrection of Our Lord.

I will have to ask the adjutant for a candle. Here, there is no possibility of buying one, but perhaps he will have a stock of them in his office.

The two officers, Lieutenant Mastacan and Lieutenant X, came to carry out an inspection before lock-up time. In the cell to which I was transferred yesterday, the bulb is not working.

What unhappiness! It occurs to me that this is a bad omen. For the first time in my life, I will celebrate the Resurrection without light – in darkness. Alone.

But the officers and adjutant Y, after several attempts, manage to get the light working.

They also brought me a small wax candle which they offered me with particular kindness.

During the several minutes of inspection, made two or three times a day, they do not speak with me. They have nothing to say to me; me, I have nothing to ask of them. Their only words to me are, 'Do you need anything?' To which I always reply, 'No!'

However, I sense in their eyes that they understand my inner sadness. They grasp the importance of the charge which condemns me, and of the responsibility that involves the leadership of a movement of more than a million souls, and which affects the fate of the nation; they understand the pain which pierces my heart for my family and for each of the hundreds and even thousands of Legionaries who, at this moment, are suffering the same bitter torments.

They also understand the humiliating position in which I find myself. The denial of freedom is one thing, whilst what is happening to me is a humiliation, a total degradation of the human person.

Without a doubt, what they do not understand are the machinations and the diabolical plans which are being hatched so as to destroy me and my movement.

They are seeking something at all costs which will lead to a heavy sentence from the court. Be it the re-opening, under whatever guise, of the Duca trial;[4] be it my involvement in the Stelescu trial;[5] be it declaring the Legionary Movement to be anarchistic and terrorist, thereby trying to condemn me in this way. A condemnation is easily obtained from such an order.

However, public opinion will be able to make out our innocence, in its soul and its conscience.

Thus, our sacrifice will grow before heaven, and God, the Supreme Judge, will hear us also.

My soul is overwhelmed by such injustices!

***

I am stretched out once again on this bed of planks. I am waiting for eleven o'clock in the evening, when people will begin to make their way to the churches. I cover myself with my overcoat. I cannot remain on my back; it hurts me to do so. But I do not know where exactly. I cannot be precise: the spine or the kidneys?

Through the cracks in the planks, through the mattress and the blanket, comes a cold draft from the paving stones which penetrates my clothes and reaches within my weakened sides.

I turn onto my right side and bring my knees up to my chin. My hips are hurting me. I feel as if a large abscess is oozing pus. I cannot rest on one side more than five minutes. But, on the other side, it is also painful.

I think of Catalina, my little girl, and her way of sleeping, her little fingers in her mouth, dreaming of Father Christmas who brings her toys.

During the Christmas holidays, I slept alongside her. Suddenly, I hear her cry in her sleep. I awaken her. 'What is it, darling? What has

---

4   Codreanu was accused of conspiracy in the murder of Duca, but was acquitted.

5   Mihai Stelescu was a member of the Legion who was also tried and acquitted of conspiracy in the murder of Duca. In 1935, he broke with the Legion and created his own political movement; in 1936, he was assassinated by the Legion.

happened?' 'Father Christmas fell off the top of the house with a bag full of toys.' Innocent angel, who knows nothing of our sufferings. She has just turned four years old.

It is perhaps eleven o'clock. I get up, I wash, I slip on my overcoat. I sit on the edge of the bed and I contemplate the silence which envelops me.

I am truly alone.

I recall: I spent two other Easters in prison, in Focsani in 1925 and in Galata in 1929.

Never, however, was I so sad, so racked by so much pain, crushed by so many thoughts.

I take my missal and set myself to read. I pray to God for everyone. For my wife, so tried and afflicted; for my mother, whom the Husi police[6] have surely visited once again and terrified; for my father, whom only God knows in which cell he is passing this night; finally, too, for my brothers, who are in the same situation as me.

Then, for the Legionary fighters, old and young, these heroes and martyrs of the Legionary faith, torn from their houses and taken to who knows what prison.

How much sadness and how many tears there will be today in hundreds of Romanian families!

I pray then for all the dead. Grandparents and relations, then for the friends who loved me and helped me in life.

I see them all, each in turn. Here is Mr. Hristache, and, finally, Ciumeti appears to me with the group of Legionary martyrs who fell at that time.

At their head, immense – I see his image as in a painting – old, 500 years old, with his long hair and his crown upon his head: Stephen the Great, Prince of Moldavia.

I pray for him, too. He helped me in so many, many battles.

There is also our General, this legendary hero, with his entourage of Legionary martyrs, with those fallen in the most recent battles.

And there, next to the General, in his green shirt, is Marin, wearing his Sam Browne belt - Marin, the hero of the Spanish plains.[7]

O Mota! Dear Brother Mota! My heart breaks when I look at you. We started out together, almost children, fifteen years ago in this

---

6   Husi is a city in the Moldavia region of Romania. It was the birthplace of Codreanu.

7   Legionaries Ion Mota and Vasile Marin went to Spain in 1936 to fight for Franco's nationalists in the Spanish Civil War. They were both killed in battle in January 1937. Sam Browne belts, named after General Sir Samuel J. Browne of the British Army in India, are a combination of a pistol belt with a garrison belt.

struggle. I see you lively and brave, facing adversity, piercing the hearts of enemies with your eyes of steel.

I see you later, overwhelmed by difficulties and by poverty, in a country where for poor Ion Mota there is no bread. For a meagre piece of bread in Romania, your great intelligence was not enough. What was wanted was the heart of a traitor.

I see you working with despair. I see you achieving tremendous success in examinations, in the press, at the Bar, on the podium.

I see you dragged into prisons. Humiliated and full of bitterness. I see your shoulders stooped and your soul saddened by so many vile attacks. I see you tremble and cry for me.

I see you leave to die. To give to this nation the supreme sacrifice. To deliver us through your sacrifice. To open with your shattered chest, with your crushed legs, the path to victory for an entire generation.

And now look at us, dear Mota. See me thrown here like a dog upon these planks. My bones feel terrible and my knees shiver from cold.

All of us, the flower of this Romania, being crushed, in who knows what jails.

Lord, I pray You, on this night of the Resurrection, to receive my sacrifice!

Take my life! Since for you, O Country, our life is not required. It is our death that you desire.

It is undoubtedly past midnight. Who knows, perhaps even later than one o'clock in the morning.

I did not hear the bells sound the Resurrection.

I light the candle and recite the traditional 'Christ has Risen!'

The people, in the towns and villages, are returning to their houses, candles lit. Our people, all our people and their families, are crying this night.

I open a tin of sardines and eat only one of them.

Since Monday night I have eaten nothing.

I drank half a jug of water.

Curled up on the mattress, I fall asleep.

WEDNESDAY, 27 APRIL

The three days of Easter have passed.

Neither my wife nor any of my acquaintances came to see me. Obviously, they did not receive permission to visit me – or perhaps they too are imprisoned, somewhere else.

How time passes slowly when you are alone! In this room, only one person enters three times a day for one minute: in the morning, at daybreak; at midday, to bring me a meal; and in the evening.

The Sun only enters for brief moments, towards five o'clock in the afternoon. And, then, in only one corner of the window.

I spend my time curled up on the edge of the bed, writing these few lines from time to time on wrapping paper.

There is neither a table nor a chair. A pencil stub, left forgotten in a pocket, is coming to its end. I can barely hold it between my fingers. The rest of the time, I lay down under the blanket.

But the humidity is penetrating both the blanket and my clothes. For the week that I have been here, I have not undressed. Nor have I been taken out into the Sun. Not even for half an hour so as to warm myself.

Yesterday, the medical officer, Holban, came to see me. What an admirable man! It was he who cared for our comrades in 1933. He knew them all.

Although I have no wish to complain to anyone, nor even to ask for something, I told him that I was getting pains at the base of my spine and in the shoulders. He replied, smiling in a friendly manner, 'That is "prisonitis" and there is no actual treatment for it.'

This night, I dreamt of Mota, who told me, 'I was released. Nonetheless, they were ashamed! Now, I am leaving for Craiova.' He goes out, gets into a taxi and drives off.

Then I dreamt of the General. He was wearing his green shirt, that which he wore on his way to Spain. He had come to my house, with my father, Colonel Zavoianu and Gameata. He exploded with laughter when he found me undressed.

***

I am always thinking, 'Where are the others? Have their families been able to find them? Are they scattered about the numerous prisons of the country? Or gathered in a concentration camp?' No matter to whom you speak, no one will give you the least bit of information.

The papers have not even mentioned their arrest. Nothing! The only thing known is that, during the night that I was picked up, they too were torn from their homes and taken to the College of Michael the Brave, where they were held for one day. Then, they were loaded into vehicles and taken to an unknown location. Amongst them are my father, Colonel Zavoianu, Polihroniade, Simulescu, Vasile Cristescu, Radu Budisteanu, Vergatti, Alexandru Cantacuzino, Cotiga and four

priests: Reverend Father and Professor Cristescu; Reverend Father
and teacher, Duminica Ionescu; Reverend Father Georgescu-Edineti;
and Reverend Father Andrei Mihailescu, who is guilty of nothing
more than being the priest of the church whose parish included our
national headquarters. He is not a member of the Legionary Movement, nor is Father Georgescu-Edineti, who is only the priest of the
students' church.

I assume that the number of those arrested in Bucharest alone is
above one hundred; professors, barristers, doctors, engineers: the
flower of the Romanian intelligentsia.

None of them is guilty in any way. They have been picked up without arrest warrants, outside the law, above the law, and against every
principle of justice.

The poor houses of the Legionaries have been desecrated so many
times that, in order to render justice, in the Romania of tomorrow, the
name 'Legionary' will have to become sacred. No public force will be
able to arrest a Legionary, nor enter his home. In the case of an offence,
only his immediate superior will be permitted to enter his home and
decide whether or not to arrest him.

There is an undeniable right to reparations which the bearers of
this name deserve, and which is so denigrated, so trampled upon and
so unjustly treated today.

FRIDAY, 29 APRIL

O Lord! How long is this day!

SUNDAY, 1 MAY

Yesterday, for the first time, I was taken out of this cellar. My legs were
sagging.

Between four soldiers, bayonets fixed, I was taken up to the Secretary's office. The Prosecutor-Captain, Atanasiu, was awaiting me
there.

I was filled with terror. I no longer have any confidence in the judiciary.

A judiciary which acts according to *orders* received, and not according to *conscience*, is no longer a judiciary.

He subjected me to a long interrogation. From six o'clock in the evening until two o'clock in the morning.

From the next room, I could hear children's voices and the sounds of family life.

I had the feeling that I would no longer know such days. And these children's voices reminded me of Catalina, 'Mummy's baby'. These voices seemed to me to be a kind of 'goodbye' given by the world to someone who would never return to it.

And the captain questioned me ceaselessly. His questions were concerned with the following points:

'Is the All for the Fatherland Party the old, banned Iron Guard?' The Legionary oaths. The meaning of the word 'Captain'. Does not the Legionary judge place himself above the state judge?

Then, were the 'secret orders' of the Home Office – published by me – related to the election campaign, or measures taken against my organisation?

What was the purpose of the Veterans' Association? Likewise the Mota-Marin Corps?

The defence of crime through promotion and the awarding of the White Cross to young, imprisoned fighters.

The secret association, 'Friends of the Legionaries'.

And, along similar lines, the 'Duca case'. Was it not me who had given the order to execute him? It was a question of trying to re-open this trial, in which I had been unanimously acquitted – the best proof of our innocence – mine, and that of the General and of other comrades.

Then, I am asked about the Senate of the Legion and the rules pronounced by the General, which gave the organisation a paramilitary character.

But here (in this Romania governed by royalist dictatorship), it is not a matter of a trial being fairly carried out; rather it is an oppression, a negation of Law, of legality, of human decency. Into which God alone can still intervene with His Power.

At two o'clock in the morning, I return, amidst the same fixed bayonets, to my resting place.

And I felt once again the absence of my darling. On the return journey, I thought once again that I would never leave this place. After which, I was overcome by a deep longing for my little girl. And, walking between the guards, I whispered endlessly, 'I will feel the absence of my darling' ...... 'I will feel the absence of my darling'.

My heart was gripped with sorrow.

Today, Monday, 2 May, the prosecutor returned. But the interrogation is finished.

THURSDAY, 5 MAY

I am still here, in this sad cell. I am alone, hour after hour, day after day.

I only see a human face when food is brought to me.

Nobody has come from home because it is not allowed.

I heard that, in another wing, in a situation worse than mine, is my poor brother, Horia. Tomorrow his trial begins. May God be with him! I pray for him. He is not a member of our Movement, and I do not even know the reasons for his arrest.

Towards four o'clock the Records Officer appeared, and listed me in the prison register as someone condemned to six months, saying at the same time that I would be freed on 15 October.

How good this would be if there were not these manoeuvers which are being directed against me!

But I believe that God will scatter them with His triumphant Light. Today, Thursday, 5 May, I felt pleasure for the first time in a long while, or rather for the second time, since I had also been pleased when my suitcase was brought to me during my first days here.

I received from home a small packet of ham, cooked fish, two portions of 'Lica' cheese and two fresh, white loaves.

And also my fur bonnet, my fur jacket, two pairs of woolen socks and some slippers. I rejoiced: a sign from my loved ones!

I could not see them, but their gesture warms my heart.

The wool-lined trousers are going to protect me from the cold.

Up until now, for fifteen days, I don't think that I have eaten more than a loaf throughout the entire time. I slept fully clothed. I have not been taken into the fresh air, even for five minutes per day. I am covered in fleas and lice which feed on me all night long.

SUNDAY, 8 MAY

Yesterday evening the Instructing Magistrate, Major Dan Pascu, came to tell me that I was going to trial for 'treason'. I was momentarily stunned! He then explained that it is a matter of the crime of possessing and publishing secret documents, touching upon the security of the state, and which appears in the Criminal Code, Article 191, under the heading 'treason'.

He subjected me to a new interrogation on the 'six orders' sent by Prefects of Police or Police Commanders to their subordinates, linking them to political and electoral dirty tricks aimed at my organisation. None of these 'orders' threatened the security of the Romanian state.

One of them, coming from the Prefect of Prahova, addressed to factory owners – the Jews of Prahova Valley – asked them to sack their Legionary workers. Another, from General Bengliu, concerning the police, had been given to me from someone in National Peasant[8] circles in Bucharest.

I am returned to my cell, my heart transfixed by arrows.

Me, the leader of the nationalist Legionary Movement, to be tried for 'treason'!

I could no longer eat anything. I fell asleep very late on my bed of bare planks, and tossed and turned all night. I awoke in the morning from my sleep, crying, 'You hear, dear Mota, I am to be tried for treason!'

***

My God, my God! How long is this day!

For hours and entire days at a time, I exchange not a word with anyone.

What must my wife and my little girl do? I heard it said that they are imprisoned in the Green House.[9] I cannot imagine why. Perhaps it is for this reason that they cannot come to see me.

And my poor father? What concentration camp can he be in? Has someone been able to see him, to bring him something to eat or something to protect him from the cold? I have no idea.

And my poor mother? How is she coping with this new burden? Because our quiet home, hidden amidst flowering apricots, has only been a place of sadness and nighttime searches since 1922. To run so many times from room to room and not meet any of your loved ones, to know nothing of their fate, when your mother's heart tells you that they are in a terrible situation. May your life not only be sighs and lamentations.

---

8   The National Peasants' Party was a moderate-conservative party in Romania between 1928 and when it was banned by the Communists after the Second World War.

9   The Green House was the Legion's headquarters in Bucharest. Green was the official colour of the Legion.

I see her face in her hands and she is crying. And I feel how the pain is breaking her heart.

O Lord, Lord, so much pain in our house! And for so many years.

MONDAY, 9 MAY

Today, Major Dan Pascu came again. And again I was taken, between fixed bayonets, to the Secretary's office.

When I went outside and I rediscovered the Sun, fresh air and warmth, I felt them as a caress. It seemed to me that, despite the fixed bayonets escorting me, the sky was blessing me.

The major tells me that the enquiry phase is finished. Now, I must choose my defence lawyers. Who could defend me!? When all of our barristers have been arrested, how can I know who will want to defend me? However, he let it be understood that I would be able to consider this until Thursday. He also told me that the prosecution brief of Captain Atanasiu had been published in the newspapers. What could my brave lads and my family say upon reading that?

How must my mother and my poor wife have cried! Me, on trial for treason.

I am returned to this room, so terribly cold. I sit, dreaming, lost in my thoughts. I have no one to advise me.

These miserable 'orders', coming from the Police, of a wholly political nature, do they affect 'the security of the state'? Do they correlate with these terrible clauses, 190-191, which mandate sentences ranging from five to twenty-five years of forced labour? I remain pensive and argue with myself, all alone.

I am going to ask for a piece of paper, and I will request the prison Governor to allow my wife to come so as to help me prepare my defence. But will she come if she is under house arrest? She, too, must act for her part. She must be tormenting herself all alone with our poor girl. Without hope from anywhere. A sole support: the Lord and the Holy Virgin.

TUESDAY, 10 MAY

Since finding myself here, in this painful situation, I have not inconvenienced anyone by asking for any kind of help. Today, I presented the following request to the prison Governor:

The Green House in Bucharest shortly after it was built.

The Green House in the late 1970s.

Sir,

I, the undersigned, Corneliu Zelea Codreanu, being a prisoner, respectfully request you to present my request to the competent military authorities so that a solution might be found.

The enquiry phase being completed, and a public case against me being prosecuted under Article 191 of the Criminal Code, I ask that my wife be allowed to visit me, since it is an urgent necessity for me to prepare for the trial, choose barristers, etc., as the trial is to be conducted under emergency procedures.

The case against me involves questions of doctrine and legal research which cannot be carried out in a short space of time.

I request, therefore, for the essentials of my defence, that I be allowed to see my wife quickly.

I request at the same time to be allowed to send the enclosed telegramme to my wife.

Rest assured of my respect.

CORNELIU ZELEA CODREANU.

FRIDAY, 13 MAY

Yesterday, Major Dan Pascu came again. It was a question of completing the last formality so as to close the enquiry phase.

To my great surprise, I was made aware of the two offences which made up the state's case against me:

1. To have armed the citizenry so as to foment civil war.

2. To have opened contact with a foreign power with the aim of fomenting social revolution in Romania.

Needless to say, neither of these accusations contains the least shred of truth.

How frightening it is to struggle against such unjust accusations! But God sees everything!

There is a suggestion that on Monday the last legal formality will be completed and that dates will be set.

Now I am awaiting Sunday. Maybe some of my family will come to see me?

I heard that my brother, Horia, was condemned to a month's imprisonment. But he is still kept locked away, in a situation worse than mine. He is greatly weakened. It breaks my heart! I pray God to come to his help also.

Yesterday evening, I had a visitor. When someone came to bring me a meal, a dog slipped between the legs of the adjutant. After the door was locked, he came out from under the bed.

He ate with me. I shared with him what I had and he ate his fill.

I spoke to him a little. Then he slept on the floor. I, too, stretched out on my mattress. I gave him the sign to jump up. He jumped up and lay next to me, after having licked my hand. Could this be a sign of hope for me?

He remained quiet. I felt the breathing of a creature at my side.

Around midnight, he wanted to go out. I lifted him up to the window and he passed out through the bars.

SUNDAY, 15 MAY

Sunday also passed, and still no one came to me.

At midday, I received chicken soup from my home in a flask, a lump of cooked meat and a white loaf. Probably brought by my poor mother and my wife. What bitterness in their souls, and what worries upon their shoulders!

I took several spoons of this warm soup, but bodily weakness and spiritual torment prevents me from eating. Thus, hour after hour, my flesh dries up on me. However, my faith in God grows in my heart. I pray each day to the Holy Virgin and St. Anthony of Padua, thanks to whose miracles I escaped death in 1934.

In these terrible moments, they are my sole consolation.

MONDAY, 16 MAY

This morning, I saw Major Dan Pascu once again and, finally, the calvary of this enquiry phase came to an end.

At each moment, I await – one never knows – other false statements to be entered into my dossier and for other false accusations be heaped upon my weakened shoulders.

He let me know that in the coming days my mother and wife will be allowed to visit me, so that I might prepare my defence.

I think: what are they going to think upon seeing me so thin? How they are going to cry!

Will they understand the torments, physical, and above all moral, to which I have been subjected?

Then, they allowed me to remain outside for an hour. It is so hot outside. I walk for several minutes, but the Sun weakened my arms and legs and I could no longer remain standing.

I sat upon a mattress and I said my prayers. After which, I stretched out, remaining like this until the hour was up.

Now, once again, I am inside. How cold it is here, and how damp. How greatly weakened I feel!

Now, it is evening time. How long the time seems since this morning! I have no one to talk to.

A small sparrow made its nest in the frame of the window. He, too, comes here to sleep. I always give him some crumbs.

I am waiting for them to bring my meal. But they, too, cannot speak to me.

It is always the Lieutenant and his adjutant who accompanies them. They, too, do not have permission to speak with me. But they behave, like the prison Governor, with a gentility which, for me, is a consolation. Poor soldier, this superior being who does his duty, carrying his orders out to the letter, but in whose eyes one sees no partisanship, no malice. Interior finesse, the school of the Romanian Army!

How beautiful it is!

TUESDAY, 17 MAY

Today, around ten o'clock, the Lieutenant came and said to me, 'Let's go upstairs, your family has arrived.'

I quickly put on my sandals and we left, this time between only two guards, seeking to help my feeble legs and thinking of how to make me look more healthy.

On arriving, my little girl came to meet me. I took her in my arms and kissed her on the cheeks and eyes, holding her close to my heart.

In this room, there was my mother and wife. They both kissed me and began to cry. My mother, the poor woman, had frozen hands.

The quarter of an hour passed as if it were a second.

I asked them about my father.

He is locked up in the concentration camp of Miercurea-Ciuc. No one has been able to see him.

My other brothers are free, except Horia, who was condemned to one month's imprisonment.

The fifteen minutes have passed already.

I do not even know what we talked about. Lizeta Gheorghiu, who accompanied them, showed me the list of witnesses and barristers. Then, they told me that tomorrow I would be taken to the Department of War.

We parted broken-hearted.

Their pain is crushing me!

FRIDAY, 27 MAY

One week ago, at four o'clock in the morning, I was awoken and taken to the Department of War, for the purpose of being able to look at the dossiers and prepare for the trial. There, I was accommodated in a more decent manner, in a room with a bed.

I met the barristers on a daily basis.

In three days, Friday, Saturday and Sunday, it was necessary to study twenty dossiers. Incredible!

In just three days, we have to find evidence for the defence: books, newspapers, parliamentary records, foreign publications. Moreover, gather together our own papers: orders, circulars, bulletins scattered who knows where. And all that made all the more difficult because your comrades, all those who worked with you, have been arrested or sent to concentration camps, or are in hiding to escape arrest. They rushed about, poor boys, these young Legionary barristers, like bees for these three days.

The famous barristers had all refused to defend me: Radu Rosetti, Vasiliu-Cluj, Paul Iliescu, Mora, even Nelu Ionescu, Petrache Pogonat, Ionel Teodoreanu, for fear of being sent to the concentration camp. Fear and cowardice!

This is why all my admiration goes out to barristers like Hentescu, Radovici, Ranetescu, Paul Iacobescu, Lizeta Gheorghiu, Caracas, Horia Cosmovici, Zamfirescu, Coltescu-Cluj. And to all this heroic youth who did not yield to any threat, and who braved and faced the tempest.

On Monday morning the first meeting took place. The military tribunal was composed of the President of the First Section, Colonel Dumitru, and of four active service officers.

Witnesses were called; we were missing all who were in concentration camps, that is to say, all those with whom I had worked closely: witnesses of the facts. We requested the adjournment of the trial and the presence of these witnesses.

The Tribunal rejected the defence request.

The charges were read out.

Full of emotion, malice and inaccuracies. Gratuitous statements, without the least proof, and lacking good faith, accuracy and the sense of honour. In the afternoon, from five o'clock until nearly midnight, I myself spoke for seven hours uninterruptedly, sweeping away one after the other of these accusations laid against me.

The following day, everything that I had said appeared, word for word, in *Universal*, except for the private hearing and the question of arms caches which the censor, out of shame, had removed.

On Tuesday, the prosecutor questioned me, and I replied point by point. In short, I had been charged with treason in virtue of:

- Articles 190 and 191 of the Criminal Code: holding and publication of secret documents touching the security of the state (based quite simply upon six orders from the police, all of an electoral nature);

- Article 209 of the Criminal Code: collusion with a foreign power, receiving instructions and assistance, with the aim of unleashing social revolution in Romania (based on one false letter, not belonging to me, and which I had never seen in my life);

- Article 210 of the Criminal Code: arming the population with the intention of fomenting civil war (based on nothing at all).

At the last moment, ten minutes before the prosecutor was scheduled to speak, and by a truly divine miracle, the author of the letter of which I was accused was found. A barrister, Marinescu, from the town of Ramnicul Valcea, on reading the letter, stated that it propounds two ideas:

1. The idea of an automated economy and of mutual exchange – words, definitions and thoughts which I have never held.

2. The idea of *economic partnership*.

He remembers having read something of such themes. He returns immediately to Ramnicul Valcea and, there, he finds the book, signed by the author. On the cover there is, as subtitle, the words 'Automated Economy', and, inside, on several pages, the author explains this new economic system.

Towards the end of the book, for about twenty pages, he argues for the other idea, *economic partnership*, for international credit, for an *international bureau*, etc. And, as a final bit of luck for us, the handwriting of the dedication is exactly the same as that on the letter of which I was accused of writing.

The barristers were jumping with joy because of this miracle and asked the President that the author, Mr. Radulescu-Thanir, be called as a witness.

Codreanu during the criminal proceedings initiated against him in May 1938.

*Four of the lawyers
defending Codreanu:
Vasile Mailat, Mircea
Vlasto, Radu Ghenea
and Horia Cosmovici.*

*Codreanu gazing out
over the Black Sea at
Carmen Sylva.*

The President rejects the request.

A group of barristers go to the home of this man. He acknowledges that he wrote such a letter. He comes to the door of the tribunal, but is prevented from entering. I raise the subject once again. 'Sir, members of the tribunal, the author of the letter for which I was accused has been revealed and is uncontested. It is Mr. Radulescu-Thanir, a collaborator of the paper, *Neamul Romdnesc*. I do not know him personally. I do not even consider the mystery of how this letter was in my home. He acknowledges that the letter is from him; that it is he who wrote it. Please bring him in so that he can explain. Take whatever steps you think suitable.'

The President rejects the request.

Finally, my seven barristers begin their defence. Impeccably so. And it is on Thursday night, at midnight, that the tribunal enters into deliberation.

I am taken to a room and, half an hour later, I am put into the Black Maria and sent back to Jilava.

I am calm and have peace of mind. I know that I am guilty of nothing.

None of the accusations thrown at me were left standing.

Here I am once again in my cell. I sleep.

Around four o'clock in the morning, I am awakened by footsteps and the sliding of bolts. I get up. Prosecutor Major Radu Ionescu, the clerk of the court, Tudor, the prison Governor and the other officers on guard come in.

The clerk of the court reads, 'The military tribunal has answered in the affirmative to all the charges. You are condemned to ten years' hard labour.'

They stay a few moments more to observe me. The major is wide-eyed and shrugs his shoulders. They all leave.

Confronted by the immense injustice which strikes at me, I remain calm and of clear conscience.

I open the book of prayers of St. Anthony at random. It opens on page 119. I read, 'May I receive calmly everything that the Lord sends, understanding that it is His Will.'

SUNDAY, 29 MAY

I miss Carmen Sylva on the sea coast. Last year, at this time, I was there and I was preparing, with Totu, the launch of the Legionary commerce.

Now, at this time of year, the traders are meeting once again and life starts up. In our work camp, weeds and briars will grow which will, little by little, cover up our work.

There, where in years past there was only action and life, health, and joy, there now grows desolation. And yet I believe that the crowds who come there during the holidays will remember me.

When I returned from the trial the next day, there were chicks in the sparrow's nest at the top of the window. The mother sparrow busies herself all day to bring them food. I watch her. Each time she returns with a full beak. There is so much chirping in their little home, so much happiness.

NOTES ON THE TRIAL

The whole time, I was held under extremely close watch, and one out of the ordinary. At the door, there were two guards permanently on duty. With me, in the room, there was an adjutant. Yet another adjutant was constantly near me.

Discussions with my defence team and the preparation of my defence, which normally are secret, took place in front of them, watched over by two police agents.

The barristers, in order to be able to see me, had to pass through – from the moment of their arrival at the courthouse – four police cordons, who subjected them to full-body searches. The rooms were full of police, who spied on the defence team, the witnesses and the officer-judges.

No two people could talk amongst themselves without someone immediately coming near to them – a third person, *an agent, a spy*. An artificial, suffocating atmosphere hovered within the walls of the Department. And even outside it.

Each barrister or witness was expecting, from one minute to the next, to be picked up, arrested and sent to a concentration camp.

Moreover, those barristers who caught the attention of the magistrates were expelled from the defence team's bench.

This was the case with barristers Radulescu and Vlasto.

Also arrested were Corneliu Georgescu, Stanicel and Popescu-Buzau.

Barristers from the province, who had registered by telegraph their intention to serve, suffered raids during the night, after which they were warned that, if they left their town, they would be arrested and sent to a concentration camp.

Finally, and with great difficulty, some of them were able to get into the court. However, at the moment when the defence began, they were no longer permitted to attend. Thus, the seats in the hall were empty.

Beyond the seven barristers arranged at the outset to conduct the case, none of the others were able to take part.

Whilst the closing speech of the prosecutor, drawn up by others and only read by him, was immediately printed in special supplements, published by order from above and under the threat of suspension for recalcitrant newspapers, and read aloud *in full* on radio, the defence case was listened to by the tribunal in an empty room, and received only a few paragraphs of press coverage.

The defence, however, was first class.

Horia Cosmovici, Hentescu, Radovici, Lizeta Gheorghiu, Iacobescu, Ranetescu, Caracas – all my admiration goes out to you, dear friends! And to all the others, you who were inseparable from me, who worked, who ran, who struggled and who agonised in waiting for the verdict.

By way of conclusion, I said, 'Sirs, you have in your hands not only my life, which I give with joy, but the honour of all the youth of Romania. I believe in the military justice of my Country.'

The tribunal had then to reply to three questions:

1. *Was I guilty of holding and publishing secret documents,* suppressed under Articles 190-191 of the Criminal Code?

Now, it was proved that the 'six' orders in question were of a political nature. They were simple orders for legal proceedings, of a purely police nature, against members of my organisation. They did not in any way broach 'the security of the state'. Similar orders had been read out in Parliament, had been published in newspapers. Every politician had such 'orders'. Mr. Maniu, in one year – he stated – had sixteen of them, which he published in a booklet.

Finally, Articles 190 and 191 of the Criminal Code appear in the chapter 'crimes against the external security of the State', and the words 'security of the state' in Article 190, in referring precisely to *external* security, means that these 'orders' could not be considered as the crime of 'treason'.

2. The tribunal had to reply to a second question: *was I in contact with a foreign state, so as to receive orders and material assistance with the aim of unleashing social revolution?* It was a claim based on a forged letter, which did not belong to me.

And where the author was revealed.

This was a question of outrageous accusations and simple bad faith (Article 209).

3. Finally, the tribunal had to give a ruling on the *crime of having armed the population with the aim of fomenting civil war*, a *coup d'etat* and so on (Article 210).

Now, we proved, by resorting to declarations of principle, to the facts and to witnesses, that the idea of fomenting civil war had never been entertained by us. And not only that, but we did not want to provoke even the least trouble, as the danger from the East was watching our every mistake, our every step.

However, the tribunal – without proof, without the least proof – replied in the *affirmative* to all of these questions, sentencing me to *ten years of hard labour*.

What an outrageous injustice!

May God accept my suffering, for the well-being and prosperity of our nation!

Pain upon pain, suffering upon suffering, agony upon agony, wound upon wound in our bodies and in our souls, fall after fall: in this way shall we conquer.

FRIDAY, 3 JUNE

(Continuation of the Trial Notes)

THE CAMPAIGN OF HATRED

I do not know if there has already been, in the public life of Romania, a man who was attacked with such bitterness, such fury and such bad faith, by the entire press and by all the offices of the Judeo-politicians, as me, since my arrest and during the entire enquiry, with the aim of softening up public opinion for my conviction.

There is no one, in the whole political history of Romania, upon whom so much hatred was concentrated. No one has been struck like me, with no possibility of defending myself and without anyone being able to take up my defence.

Buna Vestire and Cuvantui were reduced to silence from the outset, having been forbidden to appear.

Nae Ionescu was himself imprisoned in a concentration camp.

The other publications attack me with bitterness: some because of tactics, others because of orders.

Attacks which are, moreover, merely official 'communiqués' from the Home Office.

The paper which would have refused to print them, which would have dared to comment upon them and, worse still, question them, would have been banned immediately.

Notable for their venomous attacks were Curentui, Neamul Romdnesc and Capitala. That is to say Seicaru, Iorga and Titeanu.

***

THE CONDEMNATION OF THE CHURCH

I do not know if we can refer to the statement to the youth by Patriarch Miron Cristea, in which he condemns the Legionary Movement in harsh terms, in any other way. The Orthodox Church is taking an openly hostile attitude to Romanian youth.

How can one not think of the condemnation that the Catholic Church hurled, through the mouths of its bishops, at the German nationalist movement, a year or two before the victory of Adolf Hitler?

However that might be, it is painful, very painful!

To struggle for the Church of your country, on the edge of the Christian world, when the fire which is burning the churches nearby is spreading its flames towards us!

We are struggling, we are sacrificing ourselves, we are dying, blood gushing from our breasts, to defend the churches, and the *CHURCH* denounces us as 'a danger to the people', as 'gone astray', as 'alien to the nation'.

What a tragedy in our souls!

Here is a simple example so as to grasp the essence of this tragedy.

A child, who has not seen his father for a long time, runs to kiss him. When he draws close, the father looks at him coldly and hits him in the mouth, knocking out two teeth.

How can one comprehend the spiritual earthquake, the tragedy stimulated in his soul by such an unexpected blow?

The deceit, the shame, the physical pain as a response to the purest feeling, the moral anguish: which hurts the most cannot be known, but together they kill the heart of a child.

The Church of our fathers, the Church of our forebears is hitting us!

The Patriarch is also the Prime Minister, it is in his name that all these things are done and from whom so much suffering comes day after day.

Lord, Lord! What a disaster! And to what trials are you subjecting our poor soul!

So much anguish in the hearts of tens of thousands of young people, peasants, workers, students!

SATURDAY, 4 JUNE

Today, I looked at myself in the mirror and I saw, for the first time, more than ten white hairs in my beard, as white as snow. The same thing on my head.

MONDAY, 6 JUNE

Each evening, I hear singing coming from the other cells: 'God is with us, understand, peoples, and bow down'.

And then, one after the other, all the Legionary songs. The prison is full of Legionaries. They are together, I think, in groups of twenty to each room. During the day, they are free. But I cannot see them.

I have heard it said that amongst them there is Livezeanu, Talnaru and Gherghiescu.

There are more than a hundred of them. They are made up of roughly equal numbers of students, workers or peasants.

The last group are from the Ilfov county and above all from the county of Brasov. Then there are engineers from Brasov. This is all that I have been able to find out, because no one has permission to communicate or speak with me in any way.

Now, I am being taken out each morning and afternoon; at the beginning, only for one hour; now, I am left for more than one hour. I am a little better. I feel better although a dull pain bothers me nonstop at the base of my spine.

Each Thursday and Sunday, my mother, my wife, my little girl, and sometimes the barristers, come to see me.

I have enough to eat, perhaps even too much.

I am awaiting permission to have a small stove, so that I can reheat some small things, boil eggs, and make tea.

The whole day I find myself alone and I speak, in turn, to those amongst us who have already died. I see them as they were when they were alive. They stay close to me. They walk alongside me in the room. They sit themselves down on the same planks.

The majority of them have already passed through Jilava: Mota, Marin, Ciumeti, General Cantacuzino, Hristache.

They always remain at my side. And when I pray, they pray too.

I resumed reading the *Gospels* from the outset. And in spite of the passing of two thousand years, I see Our Lord Jesus Christ, such as He is described in the *Gospels*, as if He were standing ten steps away from me. I see His clothes. I see Him walk calmly in front of the Apostles, lifting up His arms while speaking with them, to bless the crowds. I see Him crushed and praying, 'O Lord! If it is possible, take this chalice from Me.'

I see how they arrested Him and how they led Him, tied, to Annas and Caiaphas.

What was in His soul, the long length of that journey?

What pain, what anguish, what overwhelming threats tormented His spirit!

What a monumental trial He had to undergo!

I see how they beat Him, how they strike Him in the face during the interrogation to which, that night, the Pharisees, the doctors and the important men of those days subject Him.

I see how they seek to confound Him by all kinds of questions. And He is silent and looks directly at each of those who surround Him. He looks them straight in the eye: will He perhaps find a friend amongst them? In such situations, a man clings to eyes redolent with friendship. A warm, friendly, understanding look gives him hope and strength.

Nothing! Everywhere the eyes of wildcats, full of hatred, perfidity and the desire to torment.

Then, I see Him, afflicted, lower His eyes to the ground,

TUESDAY, 7 JUNE

'Everybody condemned Him so that He might be put to death' (*Mark* 14:64). 'After having bound Jesus, they led Him and delivered Him unto Pilate' (*Mark* 15:1).

And in His heart there resounded the same prayer as He had uttered in the Garden of Gethsemane, 'Lord, if it is possible, take this chalice from Me.'

Yet one hope still burned in His soul: perhaps Pilate will proclaim His innocence.

Thus, He understood the struggle between Pilate and the Pharisees. But, in the end, the Pharisees emerge the victors.

Another hope destroyed. But on His face, racked with pain and tiredness, a new ray of hope arises. 'It is the Passover. It is the custom to free a condemned man.'

'Pilate is going to speak to the people. The people are surely with Me and are going to demand my freedom. I have done so much good for them. I healed so many amongst them. It is not possible that there will not be, in the crowd, at least some of those healed by Me, because everyone has heard of My arrest. They have surely come. The crowd is with Me!'

And He recalls events of barely a week ago, when He arrived in Jerusalem. The whole city received Him with flowering palms, kneeling before Him.

'The majority of the men in the crowd spread out their cloaks on the road; others cut branches from trees and lay them along the way.'

Those who went before, and those who came behind Jesus, cried, 'Hosanna to the son of David!'

'Blessed is he who comes in the name of the Lord! Hosanna in the highest.' (*Matthew* 21:8-9).

'And those who followed Me, by the thousand, during My sermons!'

His eyes lit up. If Pilate thinks to ask the people for His freedom, He is saved!

The whole problem is that Pilate should take this path.

Finally, Pilate decides. He goes out onto the balcony and cries to the assembled crowd, 'Who is it that you want me to release? Barabbas or Jesus, whom they call Christ?' (*Matthew* 27:17).

From inside, Jesus hears the question, and it seems like a hundred years to Him during the one minute he awaits the reply.

'Then once again everyone cries, "No, not Him, but Barabbas"' (*John* 18: 40). Now, Barabbas was a brigand.

'What then will I do with Jesus, called the Christ, because I find no fault in Him?'

'"Crucify Him!" they all replied' (*Matthew* 27: 22).

'But what evil has He done?'

'But they cried all the more, "Crucify Him!"' (*Matthew* 27:23).

The crowd were crying at the top of their voices, insisting that He be crucified. And it is this howling, as well as that of the most prominent priests, which won the day.

Jesus hears, and His face darkens. He cannot believe it. It seems as though He has lost His mind.

He is roughly pushed outside. The mass cries; but He no longer sees anyone or hears anything. In this moment, He no longer has power. He does not work miracles, because, from the moment of His arrest, God has removed His powers, leaving Him a mere man – like me, like all of us.

So that He might suffer as a man!

So that His suffering might be unlimited: it is only thus that He will have the power to redeem; the redemption of the mass of sins committed up to His time and beyond, up to now, up to us and unto the end of the world.

If He had remained God, He would not have suffered, and if the suffering did not take place, by what means could the sins of the world have been redeemed? It is for this that the Saviour was sent.

This is why He thought. He suffered. He hoped until the last moment, like us.

The blows, He felt like us, we men. Exhaustion broke Him as it does us. All the insults, all the injuries, all the injustices pierced His heart, just like us.

Under the weight of the blows and outrages which fell upon His head, and powerless before them, He sighed humanly, He sighed just like us.

There He is carrying His cross! I see Him falling under its weight, because our human appendages are weak, and bend under the weight of burdens. He wipes the sweat from His forehead. Around Him, there are only wild beasts. No one feels pity. No one cries for Him. They all laugh. Yet there is one small consolation: there is someone who believes in His pains. Two eyes understood Him. A heart beats, like His, at the moment of the supreme agony.

'Behind Him came two women and a multitude who were crying.'

'When they came to the place called Calvary, they crucified Him there, along with two criminals, one on the right, the other on the left.' (*Luke* 23:33). He was not an athlete able to resist, confront and fight until he was beaten.

I see Him frail, emaciated and gentle. He stretches out his thin, exhausted arm on the wood of the cross, and says to the beasts, 'Strike.'

Unfortunately; there are moments which seem like a hundred years. They take His hand. Here is the nail. He feels its first contact with His emaciated hand. Ah! The first blow! The second. He feels His arm riveted to the cross. The awful pain pervades His body. He wants to cry out, but, even for that, He no longer has the strength. He groans!

The same thing for the other hand. He stretches it out so that it is in place, whilst He remains still, transfixed by pain. His flesh and bones tremble.

Now, through the feet: here is the nail. The hammer blows are heard, one after the other. Each blow makes Him shudder. It pierces His brain.

Later, a lost voice: 'I am thirsty!' (*John* 29:28).

'It was already about the sixth hour and there were dark clouds upon the Earth. The Sun was blacked out, and the veil of the Temple was torn asunder' (*Luke* 23:44, 45).

'Lord, Lord – why have You forsaken Me?' (*Matthew* 27:46).

And then, 'Father, into Your hands, I commend My spirit' (*Luke* 23:46).

And I, on my knees, at the foot of this cross from where the soul of His Son left a human body to go to God, I pray, 'Our Father, who art in heaven'. And to the soul which is raised up, I pray also, 'Remember my loved ones. Take them under Your protection. Forgive them, give them peace. Give strength to the living and victory over their enemies, for the blossoming of Christian and Legionary Romania, and that, O Lord, your Romanian nation returns to You in the hope of its resurrection. Amen!'

Christ is Risen.

'He rose from His tomb, on the third day. I saw Him.'

'I do not believe it', says Thomas.

And Christ came amongst them. He called Thomas and says to him, 'Put your finger here and look at my hands; bring forth your hand, and put it into my side!' (*John* 20:27).

'My Lord and my God' (*John* 20:28), exclaims Thomas, after having touched with his own hands the pierced side and hands of the Redeemer.

Christ rose, sowing thereby throughout the world until the end of time, Hope; the hope that we will never perish under the burden of injustice, however heavy, weighing upon our feeble bodies.

We shall rise, we shall conquer.

Christ rose, sowing the hope of the Resurrection; the hope that our life does not finish here, with its transient sixty or seventy years; that it continues in the beyond; that we will meet our dearest loved ones, and that we will never be separated from them again.

We are going to rise in the name of Christ and only through Christ, because outside of faith in Christ, no one will rise or be saved.

THURSDAY, 9 JUNE

I dream each night. I have never dreamt as much as now. This night, I dreamt about a battle which took place in Predeal in three areas: one at the 'pump'; the other on the slope of the town that rises to Fitifoi above the barracks; the third, under my command, between the Stelian Popescu villa and the Palace Hotel, as far as the railway tracks leading to the station. No one was shooting. The battle was hand to hand. My sector swept out the enemy in a stunning way, by pushing them beyond the railway station and putting them to flight. The two other sections, with some difficulty, opened themselves a path. At the 'pump', I intervened at the last moment with my lads. The enemy was, however, repulsed by the time we arrived.

I was also on Fitifoi, where I was aiming with a gun which was more like an Aasen mortar. But I did not fire. Of those who were with me, I well remember Bordeianu and Miluta Popovici; the rest I have forgotten.

I fell asleep once more.

In front of a house, seated at a round table covered with a white tablecloth, I dreamt that I was with my father and someone else. On the table, there was a cup of black coffee. On the right, a wide valley, a few metres from us. In front of us there arose a great clay and rock hill.

All of a sudden, large blocks began to free themselves from the top and hurtle down the slope. A really green tree which was there was crushed. Then the stones began to fall onto our table. We got up and rushed to the left.

My father said to me, 'Drink your coffee.' I approached the table again, but, at the same moment, a large lump of molten earth fell onto the middle of the table, on the coffee. I moved back and immediately began to clear the earth, mixed with ashes and with brand. The women of the house came out to gather things up, upon seeing them thus covered by embers.

I noticed my father's suitcase and moved towards this heap to recover it. When I got there, one of the women was already bent over the suitcase. She was already once again covered in the earth and embers which fell, and in such a way that one could only see her feet. It was my mother! I picked her up and put her on my shoulder, whilst with my left hand, I grabbed the suitcase and pulled it out from there. Then we went down. My father came forward to help me, crying, 'The poor woman! The poor woman!' I woke up.

I fell asleep again. I dreamt of my wife, who was sleeping in a bed, then I dreamt of Nicoleta.

Going out into the street, I met Smarandescu and Horodniceanu. I asked them, 'Where is Nicoleta?' Because she had got up and left our place. And I wanted to see her. I looked for her in a particular place, but she wasn't there. I looked for a long time and, at last, I found her with my mother in a run-down house. Day broke!

FRIDAY, 10 JUNE

This morning, the first chick flew from the nest in the window. What emotion, what shuddering for him. Its first steps and its first flight in life. What a worry, what a joy for the mother! The vault of heaven is full of its calls, of its encouragements. Full, too, of chirping. Go in peace, my little one, towards holy freedom.

For the last few days, a green grasshopper has been walking in my cell. When I stretch out, it comes close to my bed. Yesterday evening, it wanted to sit on my head. I tried to make it go away. It became frightened, jumped and disappeared. This morning, I found it squashed under the mattress. I took it and cared for it for an hour. I gave it water, mixed with sugar. It drank. It recovered and then flew outside.

Towards one o'clock in the afternoon, I was called to the administration office. A new enquiry. Captain Taraneanu, from the Department of War, came to enquire himself if I had not sent from prison a manifesto in which I was inciting my men to 'vengeance'.

Naturally, it was a phantom manifesto.

I made a statement to this effect. How all sorts of plots can beat down on me!

I was sentenced for a letter which is not from me. Now, here is another.

Yet I believe the prosecutor managed to convince himself that it was not a serious affair.

This night, towards dawn, I dreamt that I was in a room full of people, so packed that I could not breathe. The windows were opened. It was the beginning of my legal appeal. Iacobescu was saying that he was going to speak for two hours. I awoke.

I fell asleep once again. I was dreaming that I was travelling on a train with my mother, my wife, my little girl and Silvia. The train tilted so heavily towards the edge that we thought it was going to turn over. So, I jumped onto the ballast, because the train was moving slowly, and I put my shoulder to it to support it. The others did the same. It came off the tracks, but it did not fall into the abyss.

MONDAY, 13 JUNE

I did not sleep the whole night. I think that my lungs are diseased at the top, as far as the shoulder blades. On both sides, I feel a dull pain and a continuous warmth. I am going to call the doctor.

Painfully, I am going to go up this calvary.

In the afternoon, the barristers came to see me, because Wednesday the 15th is my appeal to the Supreme Military Court.

They think that it will be adjourned for at least fifteen days because that is the norm.

So, we are going to lodge new reasons for appeal and request that the court grant a further delay.

I studied their reasons with them. They are of a serious nature:

1. My eyewitnesses, the men from Ciuc, those with whom I worked, were not brought forward. Not one of them!

2. I was condemned for a letter which was not from me. Its author had been found. He made a statement in which he asserted that the letter was from him, that this was true of the contents as well as of the handwriting. Thus, the author of the letter is known.

3. A false legal charge. I was charged with the crime of threatening the external security of the state, of treason, facts for which I was given an outrageous punishment. The 'orders' in question in no way touched upon the external security of the state, because they did not relate to a danger coming from a foreign power and which could undermine

a) its territorial integrity;

b) its independence;

c) its sovereignty.

4. There was not one proof, of any kind, that I had wanted to provoke civil war. Arms caches were described, but not one was shown. Where are they? What do they contain? At whose place were they found?

I am condemned on accusations without foundation.

It is unique in the annals, legally as much as from the point of view of procedure.

TUESDAY, 14 JUNE

Today, Lizeta Gheorghiu came to see me. The others are studying the files.

On this occasion, I gave her a short statement for my family, which I had written that same day in my cell.

Tomorrow, it is the appeal.

I have just finished the *Epistles of St. Paul*. I am profoundly touched. I admit that until today, I had only read some of them, and without having sufficiently studied them. I will write on this later, because it deserves an entire study.

This night, I dreamt of Gameata. He was complaining of the terrible treatment that he had suffered at Ciuc. Then I dreamt of Tell. He was being escorted. At a given moment, he ran towards Ionica's house. Finally, I dreamt of Alexandru Cantacuzino. I spoke with him in a house, but I don't remember where.

WEDNESDAY, 15 JUNE

When I had finished reading the *Gospels*, I understood that I found myself here, in prison, because of God's Will; that, despite not being guilty of anything from a legal standpoint, He was punishing me for my sins and putting my faith to the test. That reassured me. Peace came upon the torment of my soul, like a quiet evening in the countryside comes down upon the worries, the agitations and hatreds of the world. When men, birds, animals, trees and flowers, earth worked and turned over by the blade of the plough, relax.

Because I was greatly tormented.

What has my poor flesh not suffered! I do not think that I have ever endured so much suffering as now.

I did not lose the faith, nor love, but I felt for a moment that the thread of hope had been broken.

Physically tormented like a dog, my clothes are impregnated with suffering (it is sixty days now that I am sleeping fully dressed, on bare planks and this mattress. Sixty days and sixty nights that my bones are absorbing, like blotting paper, the dampness which streams down the walls and up from the floor).

For sixty days, I have not exchanged a word with anyone, because nobody is allowed to speak with me. And, moreover, I am attacked in my moral person, accused of treason, declared a stateless person, as not being Romanian either by my father or mother, denounced as an enemy of the state, overwhelmed with blows and with my hands tied behind my back. To speak the truth, without the possibility of defence.

My heart tightened at the thought of the suffering, the humiliations, the brutalities endured by my loved ones, my family and my comrades, and I felt one of the three threads which links a Christian to God break – Hope! Everything became black before my eyes. I felt suffocated.

But I succeeded in renewing it, this thread, through struggling day after day. How? By reading the four *Gospels*. When I had finished them, I felt that I once again had these three threads and that they were perfect: **Faith, Hope and Charity.**

And now, having completed the reading of the *Epistles of St.Paul*, I discovered therein decisive proofs of the reality of the Resurrection and of the power of Our Lord, Jesus Christ. What struck me is:

1. The sincerity and spiritual purity of the Holy Apostle;
2. His life, integrally Christian and without stain;
3. The danger and suffering which he underwent for Our Lord;
4. The serenity, even joy, with which he welcomed such suffering;
5. His strength in also encouraging others, so that they did not weaken before suffering and persecution;
6. His holy love, which was a rousing one, for his Christian brothers or his spiritual sons;
7. The unbeatable ardour, rarely found in the Apostles, of a belief which preached Jesus Christ to all peoples ceaselessly;
8. His great knowledge and wisdom.

In each letter he almost always begins with, 'I, the prisoner, find myself in chains because of my faith in Christ, Our Lord.'

Then, writing to Timothy: 'Come and see me quickly' (*Timothy* 4:9). He too, no doubt, wished to see someone. 'When you do come, bring a coat.' He, too, like me, was cold.

Finally, as we enter into the reading of the *Letters*, we come to these conclusions:

1. That we are not good Christians, that we are far from being so. Very far.
2. That we are Christianising our exterior, but that we are dechristianising our interior.
3. That mankind has suffered this process of dechristianisation all the long centuries down to us, with only rare flashes into the depths. Superficial Christianisation seems to have concerned mankind a great deal more.
4. The mark of our age:

We concern ourselves more with the struggle between ourselves and against other men. And hardly with the struggle between the commandments of the Holy Ghost and the desires of our earthly nature.

We are taken up with and love the victories over other men, and not the victories over Satan and sin.

All the great men of yesterday and today: Napoleon, Mussolini, Hitler, etc., were taken up above all by these victories.

The Legionary Movement is an exception, in concerning itself also, however insufficiently, with the Christian victory in man for his salvation.

Yet not enough!

The responsibility of a leader is vast.

He must not flatter his troops with earthly victories, without preparing them at the same for the decisive struggle, from which the soul of each person can emerge crowned with an eternal victory or a total defeat.

5. Lastly, the absence – at least in our country – of a priestly elite which might have maintained the sacred fire of the early Christians. The absence of a school for great improvement and a profound Christian morality.

FRIDAY MORNING, 17 JUNE

Wednesday, around five o'clock, my wife and mother came. They informed me that my appeal trial had not been adjourned as was usual. It will be held already this afternoon at five o'clock, and will continue into the night if necessary. My wife also informs me that she had been summoned to the police station at Baneasa, where they kept her from morning until 1.30, only to tell her in the end that she no longer had permission to go into our home, the Green House. On Friday, she must come and collect everything which belongs to us, and on Sunday take it wherever she wishes.

Her face was pale with frustration. Take your possessions from your own home! Take them where? Live where? Me in prison, my wife without any choice, thrown onto the streets, holding our little girl's hand.

What inhumanity! What indecency!

We three remain, asking the question: where? Where?

I give them several addresses at random. We do not have enough money to pay the rent on a house.

I explain to her that, if my appeal is rejected, I will be sent to Doftana.

She would like to come with our little girl and live in the village nearest the prison.

I tell her that I left my last testament with Lizeta Gheorghiu, and I begin to recount its contents briefly to them.

Both my wife and my mother were crying. Our little girl, barely four years old, understands nothing at all of the tragedy of this time, when the shadows of death begin to invade the thoughts of a family.

After the regulation fifteen minutes, they left.

Now, it is Friday morning. The reply to my appeal has still not come.

In our home, at this time, my wife is packing her bags and crying over her misfortunes!

But that cannot continue. We are going to return home.

Friday evening, 17 June

Half an hour ago, my barristers came to see me to tell me that my appeal had been rejected by the military Court of Appeal.

They were all saddened and defeated.

We remained together for about fifteen minutes. I asked them how the discussions had unfolded. They described them in a few words. Then, we parted. Upon returning to my cell, I sat on the edge of the bed of planks and I prayed to God, reciting the prayer: 'Our Father, Lord, may Thy Will be done'.

Sunday, 19 June

This night, about half an hour after midnight, whilst I was trying to go to sleep, I heard footsteps coming towards my cell. There is the noise of a bolt and the door opens.

The Service Lieutenant and the first guard appear. They came to tell me that it was necessary to leave for Doftana. I got up, dressed quickly, put my belongings into two suitcases and the blanket. Then, I said my prayers and left this place that had housed my suffering and torment, thinking about my unknown future.

Look after yourselves, you hundreds of Legionaries, my dear comrades who suffer within these walls!

Escorted by four guards, I arrived at the chancellery. There, I was subjected to another thorough body search. They rifled through my pockets, they fingered my collar, my sleeves, my body, my legs carefully; then, they made me take off my shoes so as to check my socks.

They looked at my bags with the same care.

I saluted Colonel Brusescu, the prison Governor and the officers who, in carrying out their duty, behaved courteously with me. There was a police major and a captain (the very same who had accompanied me from Predeal and, afterwards, to the Department of War), in whose eyes I could read a feeling of compassion for all the misfortunes bearing down on me. A sublieutenant (my old guard at the trial), also most courteous, and a police superintendent took charge of me.

I got into a taxi, having the major on my right, in the foldaway seat facing the captain, and a drill sergeant next to the driver.

About thirty metres in front of us, there was another car of policemen and, behind us, a lorry with thirty policemen.

It was two o'clock in the morning. Outside, the weather was beautiful. The lights of the capital, which we were driving towards, were reflected in the sky.

It was by the same road that I had gone, two years ago, to the village of Professor Dobre, one of my best Legionary commanders. We had stopped here one day to dine. And the memories begin to flow.

We are entering Bucharest. And the closer we get to the centre, the more familiar are the places.

The car passes along St. Stephen the Great's Avenue, a few yards from the restaurant that we had at Obor. I look and I note the dark building without the colourful Legionary signs that had covered it barely two months ago. We are following the usual route by which I returned to the Green House.

Then, Victoria Square, taking the right via Ploesti Avenue.

Other memories. This is the route by which I often went by car to Predeal, my place to relax, driven by the ever-faithful Ilarie. I was then with my wife, my little girl, and with the Legionaries. Now, I am under close guard and I am being sent to Doftana, a man condemned to ten years!

On the road, we come across a haywagon, drawn by six handsome bullocks. It is a good sign! We are approaching Ploesti. It is past three o'clock. The darkness of the night begins to diminish and, on the horizon, appear the first streaks of light.

From time to time, I speak with the major. We discover that we had both gone to the same Infantry School, twenty years before, at Botosani. He had finished six months before me. Together, we remember those days, the comrades, the officers.

We are coming into Ploesti. We are passing through the silent streets of the town. The people are asleep. We head for Campina. From behind the hills, light emerges: the captain in front of me dozed. I think of better days. Patience, on the road of suffering.

I move forward, thought carried along by hope.

After some time, there opens on our left, the beautiful and colourful valley of Prahova. The water rolls gently, slipping across the sandbanks. We go down so as to cross the bridge and then go up towards the first houses of Campina. Some women, carrying loaded baskets, are going to market.

From the centre of the small town, we take a right turn. A mile later, after a left and right, opens up, in full majesty, the valley of Doftana.

Immediately opposite, on a high hill, there is a medieval-looking castle.

It is completely surrounded by greenery. This is Doftana prison, the penal colony reserved for those condemned to forced labour, and where we are going. It is so beautiful outside! A morning of rare beauty, full of God's blessing.

The Sun rises through the trees on the hill and spreads its golden light upon the surrounding greenery, upon the water of the valley.

We have arrived. The officers and the policemen get out. The prison Governor is informed. I still remain in the car. The guards, stirred from sleep, are coming one after the other.

I am taken to the office. The Governor, the Deputy Governor and the guards are unknown to me. The last group seem to be good men; the Governor and his deputy, men of standing.

There is the same formality of a painstaking body search from head to foot. There is so much humiliation in these regulation searches!

I put up with them resignedly.

I am informed that, in this prison, the wearing of green is forbidden. The green sweater that I am wearing is removed, and I am permitted to slip on a white flannel. My green woolen gloves are also taken from me.

Finally, I am taken into the prison, which looks like a well-maintained fort. At one end, I notice a small church. God is present everywhere!

On the left, in a corridor and towards its end, there is a white room, recently painted. The ceiling is quite high, with small windows so very high up that nothing can be seen through them. It is about five metres long and three metres wide.This is my new cell, within which I am going to have to live.

At one end, there is an iron-framed bed with a straw mattress, a pillow and a blanket. On the floor, cement and two mats.

I am informed that, as I am being sentenced definitively to six months of correctional imprisonment, I will have the right to spend the entire day in the yard outside my cell. As soon as my sentencing to ten years goes before the Court of Appeal, the punishment of hard labour will be fully applied to me. It begins from the first year: the whole day locked in the cell, with only one hour of exercise.

For the moment, my family can visit me every two weeks. Thereafter, once every two months. I have the right to write to them once a week. After final sentencing, once a month.

Painful! *Very* painful! But we are going to accept this without complaint.

I stretch out on the bed. I am tired. And I am hungry. It is said that it is also as cold as Jilava. I fall asleep.

A noise awakens me. I look around me. A mouse had jumped up onto the table and had begun to nibble a small packet of provisions. I shooed it away. I dozed off once again: and once again I am awakened. I remained thus until midnight, my thoughts flying far away.

A meal of meat soup was brought to me. I ate the meat and several spoonfuls of the soup.

I walked in the yard. I returned to my cell, where I slept until five o'clock. After, I went once again into the yard. The evening meal was only a soup without meat. But I did not feel hungry.

At about seven o'clock, we had an inspection by Mr. Goranescu, the Deputy Director-General of Prisons.

In the evening, after lockup, the doctor came to examine me. Bad news. He found the upper and lower parts of my lungs, front and back, diseased.

He gave me a prescription. Calcium injections, an ointment with which to massage myself and something to improve my appetite.

My poor lungs are no longer tolerating the suffering!

After having been wounded in my moral being, after having been treated with barbarism on the physical level, I am now subjected to a third attack: the microbes are entering the fray.

But God sees and will reward!

The Prison Notes 59

Cross inscribed with the names of the Legionaries murdered at Jilava the night between 29 and 30 November 1938.

Codreanu by the sea. The quotation beneath the photograph reads, 'There will come a time when all nations on Earth will rise again, with all their dead and all their kings and emperors, to take their place before the throne of God. The highest goal of every nation is to prepare itself for this final moment – the Resurrection.'

Appendix 1:

Articles on Codreanu and the Iron Guard by Julius Evola

FOREWORD TO THE APPENDIX

Corneliu Codreanu's idea of a Preface was something 'short, military-like, and Fascist' – or so the leader of the Iron Guard stated when an Italian edition of his *Pentru legionari* (*For My Legionaries*) was going to press in 1938. How inappropriate it would be, then, to preface an appendix to his book with anything lengthier than an essential Foreword!

The reason why we have chosen to include Julius Evola's writings on Codreanu in this volume is twofold: firstly, because they bear witness to the striking appearance and character of the Captain, 'a distinctly Aryo-Roman type'; and secondly, because they bring out the most significant feature of the Iron Guard movement: its profound spirituality. According to a Romanian Legionary and friend of Mircea Eliade's, Vasile Posteuca, the day Evola met Codreanu the two of them hardly spoke of politics at all. Instead, 'they became engrossed in discussions about the inner path, mystics, and Christian doctrine'. It is this spiritual drive of the Iron Guard, which Evola stresses again and again in his articles, that has contributed to make of Codreanu's movement such a powerful exemplar for national revolutionaries the world over.

Evola's articles on Codreanu have been collected in an Italian volume entitled *La tragedia della Guardia di Ferro* (*The Tragedy of the Iron Guard*), which has served as the basis for the present translations.[1] The little historical information provided in this Foreword – including the quotes above – is likewise derived from Claudio Mutti's excellent introduction to that book. In this appendix, we hope to have collected all of Evola's most important writings concerning Codreanu and his Legionaries.

---

1   Julius Evola, *La tragedia della Guardia di Ferro* (Europa Libreria Editrice, 1996).

Julius Evola travelled to Bucharest in the spring of 1938. According to Prof. Mutti, Evola had been put in touch with members of the Iron Guard either by Mircea Eliade or Vasile Lovinescu – or possibly both.[2] What is certain is that Codreanu made such a strong impression upon the Italian philosopher that in the same year the latter published five articles on the Iron Guard in important Italian newspapers. A sixth article was released only a few months before Evola's death in *Civiltà*, the official journal of the Italian organisation Ordine Nuovo. Despite certain discrepancies and overlaps, these articles clearly testify to Evola's admiration for Codreanu as a man and leader. They also shed light on the reasons behind his murder, and provide a useful assessment of the wider significance of the Iron Guard movement.

I

AN INTERVIEW WITH CODREANU

Our car soon leaves the curious-looking centre of Bucharest behind: a collection of small skyscrapers and very modern buildings, chiefly of a 'functional' type, filled with exhibit halls and art studios reminiscent of Paris and America – the only exotic feature here being the many astrakhan hats worn by the local officials and bourgeoisie. After reaching the North station, we turn into a dusty county road skirting small buildings not unlike those in old Vienna. Extending in a straight line, this road leads us into the countryside. After a good thirty minutes, our car suddenly veers left into a country road, only to stop outside a building that stands almost alone, surrounded by fields. This is the so-called 'Green House', the dwelling of the leader of the Romanian Iron Guard.

'We have built this with our own hands', the Legionary escorting us proudly tells us. Intellectuals and artisans joined forces to build their leader's dwelling, in what almost appears to have been a symbolic and ritual action. The style of the house is Romanian: on its two sides it extends to form a sort of porch, almost giving the impression of a cloister. We enter the building and reach the first floor. Here we are met by a tall and slender young man in casual attire. His open face immediately gives an impression of nobleness, strength and loyalty. This man is Corneliu Codreanu, the leader of the Iron Guard. He is a distinctly Aryo-Roman type – like a contemporary embodiment of the ancient Aryo-Italic world. While his grey-blue eyes convey the harshness and cool will of a leader, on the whole his contour is marked by a peculiar note of idealism, inwardness, strength, and human understanding. His manner of speech is also characteristic: before answering, it is as if he became absorbed in himself and removed; then suddenly he starts speaking, expressing himself with almost geometrical precision in clearly articulated and well-constructed sentences.

'After having met an array of journalists of all nations and colours, who only knew how to ask me about strictly day-to-day politics, this is the first time', Codreanu explains, 'that – to my satisfaction – I receive a visit from someone primarily interested in the soul and spiritual core of my movement. I had come up with a formula to satisfy a journalist without hardly explaining a thing: constructive nationalism.'

'Man is comprised of an organism, which is to say an organised form, and of vital forces, as well as a soul. The same may be said of a people. The national construction of a state, while taking account of all three elements, for various reasons of qualification and heredity can nevertheless be chiefly based upon a single one of these elements.'

'In my opinion, in the Fascist movement it is the state element that prevails, coinciding with organised force. What finds expression here is the shaping power of ancient Rome, that master of law and political organisation, the purest heirs to which are the Italians. National Socialism emphasises what is connected to vital forces: race, racial instinct, and the ethical and national element. The Romanian Legionary movement instead chiefly stresses what in a living organism corresponds to the soul: the spiritual and religious aspect.'

'This is the reason for the distinctive character of each national movement, although ultimately all three elements are taken into account, and none is overlooked. The specific character of our movement derives from our distant heritage. Already Herodotus called our forefathers "the immortal Dacians". Our Geto-Thracian ancestors, even before Christianity, already had faith in the immortality and indestructibility of the soul – something which proves their spiritual drive. Roman colonisation introduced the Roman sense of organisation and form. Later centuries made our people miserable and divided; yet, just as a sick and beaten horse will still show traces of its nobility of stock, so too the Romanian people of yesterday and today reveals the latent features of its two-fold heritage.'

'It is this heritage that the Legionary movement seeks to awaken', Codreanu continues. 'It begins with the spirit: for the movement wishes to create a spiritually new man. Once we have met this goal as a "movement", we must then awaken our second heritage – the politically shaping Roman power. The spirit and religion are thus our starting point; "constructive nationalism" is our point of arrival – almost a consequence. Joining these two points is the ascetic and at the same time heroic ethic of the Iron Guard.'

We ask Codreanu about the relation between the spirituality of his movement and the Orthodox Christian religion. His answer is, 'Generally, through the fostering of a national consciousness and through personal experience, we seek to rekindle features of the religion that have often become mummified and turned into the traditionalism of a slumbering clergy. We are lucky that our nationally-based religion ignores the dichotomy between faith and politics, and can provide ethical and spiritual support without imposing itself as a political entity. From our religion the Iron Guard movement has also derived a fundamental idea: ecumenism. This represents the positive transcendence of all internationalism and abstract, rationalistic universalism. The ecumenical idea envisages society as a unity of life, a living unity, and a way of living together not only with our people, but also our deceased and God. The implementing of this idea in actual experience lies at the centre of our movement; politics, the party, culture, etc. are merely consequences deriving from this. We must rekindle this central element in such a way as to renew the Romanian man first, and then move on to build the Romanian nation and state. One particular point to stress is the fact that the presence of the deceased in the ecumenic nation – our deceased, and particularly our heroes – is not an abstract thing for us but something real. We cannot cut ourselves off from the dead; as forces freed from the human condition, they pervade and support our highest existence. The Legionaries regularly meet in small groups, known as "nests". In these gatherings they perform particular rites. What opens all meetings is the roll call of all our fallen comrades, whereby at each name those present answer with "Present!" This is no mere ceremony or allegory for us – it is a genuine evocation.'

'We distinguish between individuals, the nation, and transcendent spirituality', Codreanu continues. 'When it comes to heroic devotion, we consider what leads from one element to the next, and ultimately to the attainment of a superior unity. We deny the principle of brute and materialistic utility in all its forms: not merely on an individual level, but also on that of the nation. Beyond the nation, we acknowledge those eternal and immutable principles in the name of which one must be ready to fight and die, subordinating all things to them, with no less readiness than if he were fighting for his own existence and right to life. Truth and honour, for instance, are metaphysical principles that we consider higher than our very nation.'

We learned that the ascetic character of the Iron Guard movement is not abstract, but rather something concrete and actually put into practice, so to speak. For instance, a rule is made for fasting: three days a week, around 800,000 men practice the so-called 'black fast', which consists in abstinence from all food, drink and tobacco. Likewise, prayer features prominently in the movement. The elite assault corps that bears the name of the two Legionary leaders fallen in Spain, Mota and Marin, even abides to the rule of celibacy. We ask Codreanu to explain the precise meaning of all this. Pausing to focus for a moment, he answers, 'There are two aspects involved. To grasp them, we must bear in mind the dualism that marks each human being, which is comprised of a naturalistic material element and a spiritual one. When the former prevails over the latter, we have "hell". Every form of balance between the two is then bound to be precarious and contingent. Only complete mastery of the spirit over the body can serve as the normal condition and prerequisite for genuine strength and heroism. We practice fasting because it fosters a condition of this sort by loosening bodily bonds, favouring self-liberation and the self-affirmation of pure will. When we add prayer, we ask the powers on high to join our forces and invisibly support us. This leads us to the second aspect in question: it is sheer superstition to believe that in all struggles only material and purely human forces are what count; for on the contrary, invisible, spiritual powers are also at play that are no less efficacious than the former. We are aware of the positive character and importance of these forces. For this reason, we have given the Legionary movement a clearly ascetic character. The ancient knightly orders also abided to the principle of chastity. I should note, however, that in our case this principle is only limited to the Assault Corps, not least because of practical considerations: for those who must be entirely committed to fighting and have no fear of death should not be encumbered by family duties. Besides, one can only stay in this unit up to the age of 30. One principle, though, always remains valid: on the one hand, we have those who only know "life" and thus search for prosperity, wealth, well-being, and opulence; on the other, those who aspire to something beyond life: glory and victory in a struggle that is internal as much as external. The Legionaries of the Iron Guard belong to the latter category. Their warrior asceticism is rendered complete by one final norm: the vow of poverty made by the elite of the leaders of the movement, who follow the precept of renouncing luxury, empty diversion, and so-called mundane entertainment – an invitation to genuine change we make to each Legionary.'

Julius Evola

(*Originally published in* Il Regime Fascista *on 22 March 1938.*)

II

NATIONALISM AND ASCESIS: THE IRON GUARD

Bucharest, April

It is a fact that the new national movements are marked by various traits presenting certain analogies with the ideas that underlay Medieval knightly orders. It is undeniable, for instance, that an attempt is being made in Italy and Germany to shape youths according to a warrior, ascetic lifestyle. In the columns of this paper we have often taken the opportunity to describe the kind of initiatives which National Socialism is systematically attempting to carry out through the establishment of its so-called 'Order Castles', or *Ordensburgen*, and corresponding practices for the selection of a new group of future leaders.

Any attempt to fully implement a similar project, however, both in Italy and in Germany is bound to face certain difficulties due to the fact that the conditions that shaped the civilisation of the Middle Ages are no longer present. The new orders are being established in the name of a strong nationalist persuasion possessing a mystic content that certainly does not coincide with the prevailing religion, which by its very nature is universalistic and supra-national. In Germany the situation is made even more difficult by the religious schism that has led to a multiplicity of religious confessions and by racialist-heathen tendencies that oppose Christianity without being founded however on any genuine principles or authentic spiritual tradition.

In the context of these tendencies towards a new 'order', a movement which appears most interesting and is less widely known is the Roman Legionary one of the so-called 'Iron Guard', headed by

Corneliu Codreanu. This movement was started in 1927 and has led to the foundation of a number of political parties, the latest of which, 'All for the Fatherland', has recently been disbanded by Codreanu himself for reasons we shall outline. The chief characteristic of this movement lies in its essentially religious premises. It presents itself as a movement of national renovation and at the same time as a tendency towards the re-embracing in a living form of the spirituality of the Orthodox religion. As this religion is structured on a national basis, such tendencies in Romania are not hindered by the kind of obstacles other nations are facing. It should be noted, however, that the official representatives of Romanian religion, as is frequently the case, have only preserved the outer shell of the religion and are often cut off from those who instead embody its spirit. The most striking illustration of this is the fact that the current Patriarch is the head of a cabinet set up by the King, who is well-known to harbour hostile feelings towards the 'Iron Guard'.

Whatever may be the case, the religious element constitutes the central core of Romanian Legionarism, which has derived from it a need to create a new man by means of specific ascetic practices. Many a reader will thus be surprised to discover that over 600,000 men – for this is roughly the number of Codreanu's followers – systematically practice not only prayer, but even fasting: three times a week the Legionaries are asked keep the so-called 'black fast', which consists in not eating, drinking or smoking.

Codreanu himself, during one of our conversations, explained the meaning of the above practice in the following terms: the complete supremacy of the spirit over the body must be ensured and fasting is one of the most effective means to this end; by loosening the bonds formed by the most natural, material part of man, fasting also fosters a favourable condition for evoking invisible forces – forces from on high which are evoked through prayer and ritual. And in all tests and struggles – despite what 'positive minds' may believe – these forces play a part no less decisive than that played by visible, material and purely human forces.

Within Codreanu's Legionary movement there exists a sort of assault militia which includes around 10,000 men and is named Mota-Marin, after the two Romanian Legionary leaders who fell in the anti-Bolshevik struggle in Spain. This corps abides to the rule of celibacy – another feature it has in common with ancient knightly orders. Again, the explanation Codreanu gave us for this is first of all that this unit must be ready to face death at any moment, and so should be free from family ties; secondly, he drew a distinction between those whose vocation must be victory and glory and those who rather belong to the world and strive after prosperity, well-being and pleasure. Hence – and this is another distinguishing characteristic of the movement – the leaders of Romanian Legionarism take a vow of poverty and never go to meetings, theatres, dance halls or cinemas.

One specific element Codreanu's movement has derived from the Orthodox religion and which also has political implications is its 'ecumenical' ideal. This consists of a particular sense of community, which is not confined to a feeling of organic mutual connectedness among men belonging to the same people, but also includes a feeling of communion with the dead and with God. The idea of a presence among the living of the forces of the dead, particularly heroes, is especially felt in the Romanian Legionary movement and undoubtedly reflects well-known aspects of pre-Christian spirituality (the relationship between the *gens*[1] and its ancestors and founding heroes). This engenders a rite that corresponds to that practised in certain Fascist ceremonies, but which here possesses a particular and almost technical, we might say, evocational intention. The Legionaries regularly gather in small groups, which take the name of 'nests'. These gatherings are intended to foster the spiritual formation of individuals and mutual understanding between them, and to a lesser extent also aim to keep members in touch with one another, to circulate news, and to serve various practical purposes, depending on the circumstances. Those who have assembled in a 'nest' practice rites and prayers together. The opening rite at each meeting is the evocation of dead heroes. Their names are read out and each is followed by a shout of 'Present!' on the part of all those gathered, who stand in line at attention. The name born by the first organisation of the movement is itself revealing: 'Legion of Michael the Archangel'. All these men have taken a stance; they are fighting for a political ideal and are ready to sacrifice their lives for renewal and the national, 'fascist' reconstruction of the Romanian people.

Corneliu Codreanu has personally struck us as one of the brightest and most loyal characters we have had the chance to meet among those active in nationalist movements abroad, and one of those most deeply pervaded by profound idealism and a noble indifference towards himself.

In the face of the abrupt autocratic intervention of King Carol, in order to avoid having to engage in a battle whose terrain had been prepared by his adversary, Codreanu has favoured a 'strategic retreat' by disbanding his party, 'All for the Fatherland', and confining the

---

1   Clan.

action of his movement to the invisible formation and spiritual train-
ing of the multitude of people who have lately joined his ranks. This
does not change the fact that Codreanu's movement possibly remains
the only decisive one to ensure a bright future for Romania. The most
happy scenario would be for the King also to realise this and overcome his own rather marked idiosyncracies in order to accept a collaboration with the 'Iron Guard' – for they themselves are in favour of
the monarchical regime.

It is well known that Romanians generally do not enjoy 'good
press', so to speak, when it comes to their character and moral stature.
Whatever the extent to which this may be true, it is nonetheless certain
that in basing his national reconstruction programme on an attempt
at spiritual regeneration and on an ascetically reinforced 'soldierly'
life permeated by spirituality, Codreanu has shown he has identified
what must be the focus of all efforts and what is bound to put the
deepest vital and moral capacities of the Romanian people to the test.

(Originally published in Corriere Padano, *Ferrara, 14 April 1938, pp. 1-2.)*

III

IN THE AFTERMATH OF CODREANU'S MURDER: THE TRAGEDY OF ROMANIAN LEGIONARISM

With the killing, or rather – to quote an expression used in the *Popolo d'Italia* – with the massacre of Corneliu Zelea Codreanu and of the other leaders of the 'Iron Guard' who had been arrested together with him, the tragedy of Romanian nationalism has now reached its final stage. One of the most noble and generous figures active in the anti-Jewish and 'fascist' front in Europe has passed away. The situation in Romania appears as murky and bleak as it has only been in a few other moments of the country's history.

It is impossible to make sense of recent political developments in Romania without bearing in mind that they were chiefly triggered by the antagonism between the central government and the movement of the 'Iron Guard'. All other forms of opposition played only a minor and accessory role, which nonetheless can in no way be understood on the basis of ordinary logic, and which reveals the influence, directly or indirectly, exercised by supra-national powers. For, now that Prague has fallen, is Romania not the only country in central-eastern Europe of considerable economic and strategic importance to still leave a sufficient margin for the operations of so-called 'Western democracies', as well as those of Israel[1] and its masked acolytes? One should not forget the fact that the final and decisive phases in the aforementioned conflict significantly coincide with the occurrence of

---

1   As the state of Israel did not yet exist at the time Evola was writing, clearly he is referring to the Jewish people rather than to Israel as a political entity.

two international events, the *Anschluss* and the Munich Pact,[2] as if to form their counterpoint.

Ever since 1920, when he was just over the age of twenty, Corneliu Codreanu had provided the outline for a constructive model of Romanian nationalism. He had denounced the Jewish peril and the enslavement of Romania under the yoke of Jews and political schemers who knew no faith or fatherland. Organising some action squads, he had taken to the streets to fight against Communism: he had torn down the red flags raised by workers in revolt in their factories, and smashed the Judeo-Communist printing houses of newspapers which specialised in insulting the Church, state, and army. Since then, the struggle has carried on unceasingly. As those loyal to Codreanu suffered persecutions, violence and defamatory attacks of all kinds, the number of his followers and sympathisers strikingly increased. Suffice it to mention the fact that in 1925, when Codreanu was forced to defend himself in a trial in which he was accused of having personally murdered his comrades' executioner – a charge of which he was soon acquitted – 19,300 lawyers from all over the country officially offered to plead his case.

As the Iron Guard movement grew, the parliamentary and party-based democratic system – which Codreanu had so violently opposed – became increasingly crisis-ridden. Its inadequacy and corruption grew more and more evident. The international Right-wing press gave a cry of joy at the beginning of this year when Goga[3] was called into power by King Carol. This was heralded as the start of a new authoritarian and 'fascist' age for Romania, as the building of a new strong and totalitarian regime destined to free the country from dark forces, both internal and external – as a regime, that is, which on an international level would have joined the front of anti-democratic, anti-Jewish and anti-Communist powers. People formulating similar conjectures and harbouring such hopes, however, were unaware of the background to these events. Besides, certain positive possibilities still remained open then which later events soon ruled out.

2   The *Anschluss* refers to the annexation of Austria, and its subsequent incorporation into the Third Reich, by Germany in March 1938. The Munich Pact was the September 1938 agreement between the Reich, France and Great Britain to allow Germany to annex Czechoslovakia.

3   Octavian Goga was appointed Prime Minister by the King on 28 December 1937 and remained in office until his resignation on 10 February 1938. He was granted dictatorial powers, passed the first anti-Jewish laws, and modeled his own movement on the Iron Guard, at least outwardly, in order to divert followers away from Codreanu. In spite of this, Goga was never anything more than a vehicle of the King's own power and desires.

One fact overlooked at the time was that, through a sort of tactical convergence, most of the forces that had previously sided with the front of subversion had now joined that of order, in order to carry on their game more easily. These new guardians of 'Romanicity' and of the authority of the state crucially harboured a firm and rabid enmity towards Codreanu's movement – when, had they been in good faith, they logically ought to have seen in Codreanu and his powerful movement their most precious ally. As for the Jewish question, this was carefully bypassed. Let us quote the words of Codreanu himself, as they appear in the volume entitled *The Iron Guard*,[4] which has most recently been published in Italian (in the *Europa Giovane* series, Casa Editrice Nazionale, Turin and Rome, 1938):

> In 1919, 1920, 1921, the entire Jewish press was assaulting the Romanian state, unleashing disorder everywhere, urging violence against the regime, the form of government, the church, Romanian order, the national idea, patriotism. Now, as if by a miracle, the same press, controlled by the same men, changed into a defender of the state's order, of laws; and declares itself against violence. While we become: 'the country's enemies', 'extremists of the Right', 'in the pay and service of Romania's enemies', etc. …
>
> We have endured outrage after outrage, ridicule after ridicule, slap after slap, until we have come to see ourselves in this frightening situation: Jews are considered to be defenders of Romanianism, sheltered from any unpleasantness, leading a life of peace and plenty, while we are considered enemies of our nation, with our liberty and life endangered, and we are hunted down like rabid dogs by all the Romanian authorities.

What the Goga cabinet truly stood for was an attempt to bring the Iron Guard down. Given that the nationalist movement was gaining momentum, an attempt was made to remove this threat by offering the nation a surrogate nationalism, something which outwardly mimicked the ideals and goals of the Legionary Guards but effectively – by means of specific forms of control – was always destined to remain part of the 'other world'. Hence, Goga was chosen, as he was both anti-Semitic and an adversary of Codreanu's. Patriarch Christea was appointed in order to show that the religious forces which were

---

4   This is the book which has been published in English as *For My Legionaries* (Reedy, West Virginia: Liberty Bell Publications, 2003). The passages following are taken from this translation.

crucial to the propaganda and idealism of Codreanu's nationalism were being heavily represented on the other side. General Antonescu, a reputedly nationalist and authoritarian figure who was called to join the new government as War Minister, was seen as an ally and substitute. And yet, the game soon proved to be a dangerous one, leading to opposite results from those hoped for.

The Goga cabinet was not taken as an end in itself; rather, it was regarded as a preliminary step inevitably destined to lead to other phases, culminating in the final triumph of true nationalism, which continued to be identified with Codreanu's movement. It was soon realised, however, that a device had been built which was ready to go off at any minute, and that something needed to be done. With no plausible justification, the Goga cabinet was dissolved from one day to the next. The elections it had promised, and in which Codreanu's movement would no doubt have triumphed, sweeping away its surrogates, were revoked. Orders were instead given that all parties be disbanded and a new constitution drafted, for which a *pro forma* plebiscite was held.

This was only '*pro forma*' because Codreanu had immediately withdrawn as soon as he had realised that the game had changed. Without waiting for the authorities to do so, he had spontaneously disbanded his party ('All for the Fatherland') and ordered his followers to abstain from voting in the plebiscite. Codreanu did not wish to engage in a battle whose terrain had been prepared by his adversary; in particular, he wished to avoid having to say *yes* or *no* to a *fait accompli* such as the Constitution. The latter had been developed directly by the monarchy and was chiefly marked by a particular concentration of powers in the hands of the sovereign. Now, Codreanu himself was a monarchist: while there is hardly a charge that has not been levelled against him by his enemies, no one has ever gone so far as to accuse him of wishing to establish a new dynasty.

In the months that immediately followed the promulgation of the new Constitution, not all hope appeared to have been lost. People believed, that is, that a new form of collaboration had possibly been found between Codreanu's nationalist, totalitarian movement and the new authoritarian and anti-democratic system centred on the monarchy.

Fascist Italy was already there to illustrate the fruitfulness – and feasibility – of such a synthesis.

Instead, what occurred was exactly the opposite. This clearly goes to show that what was at play were not any sincere feelings of love for the idea of the Romanian nation and of its unity, but rather forces of a very different kind, operating via intermediaries who were more or less conscious of their role. A moment of tension was reached, but things came to a standstill; so on the one hand the Legionary movement increased its work of propaganda, while on the other those who had done their best to remain faithful to the government started turning towards Codreanu. Among these was General Antonescu himself, who in the end was discharged and arrested.

A declaration of war ensued. The government launched the first attack immediately after the *Anschluss*, fearing that this event might trigger an insurrection. This is the reason why Codreanu was arrested. At first it was recalled that he had once insulted a minister; then he was accused of high treason. So little evidence in support of this charge was found, however, that requests for either the death penalty or life imprisonment were dismissed, and Codreanu was sentenced to ten years in prison. This resolution, too, was ill-planned, for it only served to inflame people's spirits, leading to a period marked by clear acts of terrorism, retaliation and direct action against those held to be most responsible for the ills of the Romanian nation. The 'death battalion' created by Codreanu – the one named after Mota and Marin, the two Iron Guards fallen as Legionaries in Spain, and whose members abide to the rule of celibacy – then went into action, carrying out the orders of a mysterious 'national tribunal'. This unrest particularly increased following the capitulation of Prague and Italy's more explicit siding with the anti-Semitic front. Reaction too, however, became more violent and ruthless, until the final phase was reached with the assassination of Codreanu and his leading associates, and the arrest of Antonescu.

Now that the irreparable has happened, no transition or settlement is possible. All ideas aside, the mutual hatred and thirst for vengeance which have arisen have no chance of being appeased. It is difficult to tell what tomorrow might bring in Romania.

Whatever the solution may be, the fact remains that a noble and generous leader has fallen, a victim to dark forces. This was a man whose loyalty and sincerity had the power to persuade all those who approached him; a man whose words of farewell when we parted for the last time were, 'Whether you are headed for Rome or Berlin, let all those who are fighting for our ideals know that the Iron Guard is unconditionally on their side in the unrelenting struggle against democracy, Communism, and Judaism.'

(Originally published in Corriere Padano, *Ferrara,*
6 December 1938, pp. 1-2; the same article was
republished in Lo Stato, *Rome, December 1938.)*

IV

CAUGHT IN THE ROMANIAN STORM: VOICES FROM BEYOND THE GRAVE

Our meeting took place in March. It was in the 'Green House', the headquarters of the 'Iron Guard'. 'We have built this with our own hands', we were informed – not without some pride – by the Legionaries who had come to pick us up in Bucharest and were now accompanying us. We crossed a sort of guardroom. Then on the first floor a group of Legionaries made way for us. A slender young man warmly approached us. His frank and honest face, and especially his azure-grey eyes, gave a curious impression of resoluteness and contemplativeness. This was Codreanu, the leader of the 'Iron Guard' and chief exponent of Romanian nationalism and anti-Semitism. He invited us to take a seat. His Legionaries withdrew. A woman – 'My wife', Codreanu explained – with a silent smile brought me a small plate with some fragrant jam and a glass of water, according to Romanian custom. Codreanu apologised. 'We cannot take anything today. It is a day of fasting for the Legion.' Indeed, it is one of the rules of the 'Guard' to keep a strict fast twice a week – with no drinking, eating or smoking allowed ('black fast', they call it).

At the time we were still in the aftermath of the fleeting appearance and disappearance of the Goga cabinet, of the new Constitution – which had been approved through a *pro forma* plebiscite – and of the new authoritarian line embraced by the central Romanian government. Certain possibilities still remained open then which later events were to rule out. People believed that once the new Constitution would have brought an end to the democratic party system, a collaboration between the government and Codreanu's Legionary movement would have been possible and would have brought fruitful results.

We were still waiting for things to happen. Yet those who were aware of what was at work behind certain events harboured few illusions.

Having received some information from Romanian friends who helped organise our meeting, Codreanu expressed genuine satisfaction at not having to confine his conversation – as was the case for him with many journalists – to the formula of 'constructive nationalism', but rather at being free to talk about the spiritual foundations of his movement.

'In each living being three aspects may be distinguished', Codreanu started telling us, 'that of the body as form, that of vital forces, and that of the spirit. Similarly, each political movement which seeks to bring renovation, despite being a unitary whole, may lay greater emphasis of what corresponds to a particular one of these aspects, without of course ignoring the other two, depending on the heritage, tradition and particular qualities of its stock. Fascism, I believe, stresses "form" above all, in the sense of that informing power that shapes states and civilisations, in line with its great Roman legacy. What stands out in National Socialism is the more biological element, the myth of the blood and race, which corresponds to the "vital" part of each being. The Iron Guard instead wishes to take the purely spiritual and religious aspect as the starting point for its work.'

'One must draw a distinction between "party" and "movement", as well as between the merely political aspect of a movement and its internal one', Codreanu explained. 'A party is simply a way of appearing in given conditions in the course of one's struggle. We have had several parties. At this time, I have deemed it best to disband our last one, called "All for the Fatherland", without ever thinking of ending the movement. When it comes to the latter, what we consider an essential duty is not to draw any new platforms, but rather to create and define a new man, a new being. The rest will follow as a consequence.'

'This task we envisage on a religious and ascetic, as well as a heroic level. Herodotus called us "the immortal Dacians", mentioning faith in the immortality of the soul as one of the defining traits of our stock. Despite the miserable state which the Romanian people finds itself in today, stricken as it is by enduring enslavement, corrupted by political schemers, and oppressed and exploited by the Jew, this ancient heritage lives on. It must be reawakened. It must become our focus. Along with it our other heritage must speak, that of Rome – this maker of states.'

'We know the dominant type of man in Romania nowadays,' Codreanu excitedly explained. 'We have already encountered him in history: under his rule, nations have perished and states have been destroyed. For this reason, the centrepiece of our programme is man – the reforming of man – not our political platform. Our "Legion" we envisage as a school of life. The name it first had was a mystic one: "Legion of Michael the Archangel". When this school will have managed to produce and spread a new kind of man possessing the qualities of an ascetic, soldier, believer and fighter, then Romania will have found someone capable of giving it a new form, of destroying the very roots of the Jewish idea, of sweeping away what remains of an old world, and finally of infallibly winning the future by holding sway over the young. Our enemies know this and hate us for it. Their hatred increases the more we withdraw from the surface to work on those deep and yet uncontaminated strata of the Romanian people, there where they cannot catch or defeat us – for in these strata alone does the voice of truth resound.'

The Iron Guard actually had – and still has – many of the traits of an ancient Order, as opposed to those of a political party. A special assault corps, named Mota-Marin, after the two Legionary leaders fallen in Spain (the 'Iron Guard' was among the first forces to shed their lives in the anti-Bolshevik struggle in Spain), and which at the time was 10,000 men strong, abides to the rule of celibacy, for no domestic preoccupation is to diminish the Legionary's readiness to sacrifice himself and even die. The leader must also avoid any display of wealth, as well as all things 'mundane', such as dances and the theatre. One of the characteristics of the movement is its structuring in 'nests'. These consist of cells with few men which are spread across the country; its members are spiritually trained and put to the test. A crucial feature of these 'nests' are the common religious rites and particular mystical-heroic evocations that take place within them. As already mentioned, Codreanu had imposed the rule of fasting upon his entire Legionary corps, which at the time – excluding its sympathisers – was reckoned to be of around one million men. In the course of our conversation, Codreanu also explained the reasons behind such a policy. 'In us there are two elements: spirit and matter. These are difficult to balance. The subordination of the former to the latter is "hell". The subordination of matter to the spirit instead represents the normal condition of man, and a prerequisite for all genuinely ethical and heroic living. Fasting is one of the many methods that foster this supremacy of sheer spiritual power over corporeality. This is the first point in our programme.'

'Secondly', Codreanu continued explaining, 'I believe that in all struggles and for all victories, what proves decisive are not only material, tangible powers, but also and especially spiritual, extrasensory ones that transcend man. These mysterious powers are those of the dead, of our heroes, which are linked to our earth and blood; above them are divine powers. The evocation – an effective, not merely allegoric evocation – of such powers is one of the precepts of Legionarism. It proves more efficacious, however, if it is made in a condition of spiritual freedom and supremacy – a condition which fasting fosters. Rites and fasting, therefore, are included alongside other ethical and political practices as part of the tasks undertaken in our "nests".'

Codreanu then moved on to discuss the related question of his hierarchical ideal of the nation.

'Three elements exist: the individual, the nation, and God. The individual must be integrated within the nation. The nation, within divine law. We regard the nation as an organic whole. It includes the living and the dead, human forces as well as divine. It is both an ethnic and mystical entity. The individual must integrate himself within the laws of the nation, and the nation within the laws of God. What we are taking up here is the concept of ecumenicity found in our tradition, namely the Orthodox Christian religion.'

'From this point of view, we perhaps find ourselves in a more favourable condition than nationalist movements in other countries, which have to struggle against either a variety of religious confessions or the universalistic character of a supra-national Church. The Orthodox Church is instead a national one. Hence the possibility for politics and religion to intertwine, and to develop heroism not merely in the name of worldly glory and one's patriotic duty, but also in the name of divine mysticism. I see the true destiny of our people as lying not in time but in eternity. Political achievements, culture, struggles and national greatness are means, not ends in themselves. The ultimate goal is not life but resurrection.'

'For this very reason, we acknowledge the validity of laws based on honour and transcendent principles that go beyond mere material or collective usefulness. I would never adopt a policy advantageous for my country if it betrays the laws of honour. I laugh at all the alliances we consider useful nowadays: I believe that Romania must at all cost side with the anti-Bolshevik, anti-Jewish and anti-Marxist powers.'

'I have been anti-Semitic since 1919-20', Codreanu continued explaining when we brought up this particular point. 'I would argue that the anti-Semitic struggle is a matter of life or death for Romania. Things here have reached a point where a solution is no solution at all unless it is a radical one. With the chameleon-like qualities so typical of him, the Jew will take any form, depending on circumstances, as long as it is the one that best enables him to continue his ruthless fight against us and his petty game with others. We have thus seen the very same Jewish or Jewish-funded press promote Communism and spur people to rise in revolt against the state, the army, and the Church until recently; then praise democracy; and now, finally, pose as a champion of the established order and of the law, denouncing us as enemies of the state and of Romanicity on the payroll of foreigners. This is tragic but true.'

'Our anti-Semitism is concrete and political, without of course forgetting about higher points of reference, through which the true extent of the Jewish peril and of Jewish action can be discerned. It is both concrete and political because of the huge percentage of Jews in our everyday life, of the Jewish invasion of free Romanian trade and finance, and of the Jewish enslavement and colonisation of entire Romanian districts. What is more, we are aware of all that Israel is doing to sever the deepest roots of our race, first of all by distancing it from God via means of all sorts of materialist and atheist ideas; and secondly, by distancing it from the earth and from tradition, and by corrupting its body and soul, once it has thus been cut off from the forces on high. All those who share this "ecumenical" view of the nation which I mentioned just now are aware of the extent of this peril and realise that without the complete elimination of the Jewish hydra, any form of national reconstruction – particularly at our hands – will be impossible.'

The events which were destined to unfold, leading to the massacre of Codreanu himself, are all the more tragic because they suggest that dark forces were at work. For the Iron Guard movement, aside from being nationalistic, corporatist, anti-democratic and authoritarian in nature – as the Roman government sought to be in its new phase – was also in favour of monarchy. If Legionarism was ever spared any charge by its enemies, it was that it planned to overthrow the old dynasty and establish a new one. These are the words Codreanu himself used: 'We are all in favour of monarchy. It is just that we cannot renounce our mission and the struggle we are conducting against an old and corrupt world in the name of a new one.'

He had added, 'We find ourselves today in the situation of men who have first seized the front line of the trenches, then the second and the third, and our adversary, shut up in his retreat, in the safety which it offers, is now firing at us, not knowing that we would like nothing better than to come to his aid against his real enemies. But despite all that they will do to stop us, the new Romania will win.'

We discussed many other things, as the weak light of dusk slowly spread across the squalid expanse of the Romanian plain. Finally, Codreanu left us a badge of his most recent party as a keepsake: a black disk studded with a series of silver crosses, not unlike a grid. 'These are prison bars', he remarked with a smile – unaware that his jest was sadly to become true. He then offered to accompany us across the city in his own car, with no concern for the sensation this might have stirred. Nor, on our part, did we heed the warning given by our legation, which had told us that anyone who had met Codreanu would be expelled from the Kingdom within twenty-four hours. Taking his leave from us on the threshold of our hotel, knowing that we were to continue our journey across Europe, Codreanu told us, 'In Berlin or Rome, send my regards to all those who are fighting on our same front and let them know that the Iron Guard will unconditionally be on their side in the future struggle against Judaism, Bolshevism, and false democracy.'

(Originally printed in Quadrivio, *Rome, 11 December 1938, p. 6.)*

V

THE TRAGEDY OF THE ROMANIAN IRON GUARD: CODREANU

Bucharest, March 1938

The car is leading us outside the suburbs of the city via a long, wretched B road, under a grey and rainy sky. It suddenly turns left, enters a country lane, and stops in front of a small villa with a sharp outline: the 'Green House', the headquarters of the 'Iron Guard'. 'We have built this with our own hands', the officer of the Legionaries who is accompanying us tells us, not without a certain pride. We make our way into the building, walk across a sort of guardroom, and reach the first floor. A group of Legionaries make way for us as we are approached by a tall and slender young man, with an uncommon expression of nobleness, frankness and energy imprinted on his face. His azure-grey eyes and open face reveal a genuine Roman-Aryan type; mixed with his virile traits there is also something contemplative and mystical in his expression. This is Corneliu Codreanu, the leader and founder of the Romanian 'Iron Guard', he who is being called an 'assassin', 'Hitler's henchman' and an 'anarchist conspirator' by the world press, for since 1919 he has been challenging Israel and the forces more or less in cahoots with it that are at work in Romanian national life.

Of the many national leaders we have met during our journeys across Europe, few, perhaps none, have made such a favourable impression on us as Codreanu. With few were we able to converse with such a perfect agreement of ideas; in few we found the same capacity to rise so resolutely from the plane of the contingent and to base the desire for political-national renewal on premises of a genuinely spiritual nature. Codreanu himself did not conceal his satisfaction in meeting someone he could speak to without confining his conversation to the stereotypical formula of 'constructive nationalism' – a formula which fails to grasp the essence of the Romanian Legionary movement.

Our meeting took place at the time of the fall of the Goga cabinet, of the direct intervention of the King, of the promulgation of the new Constitution, and of the plebiscite. We were aware of all the real details behind these upheavals. In a lucid synthesis, Codreanu contributed to the picture we had of the situation. He had much faith in the future, and, indeed, in the imminent victory of his movement. If the latter hadn't reacted or shown any signs of opposition, this was for precise tactical reasons. 'If there had been regular elections, as Goga had in mind, we would have won with an overwhelming majority', Codreanu told us, verbatim. 'But faced with the alternative of saying yes or no to a *fait accompli* such as the Constitution, a project inspired by the King, we refused to take up the fight.' Codreanu also added, 'We have first seized the front line of trenches, then the second and the third, and our adversary, shut up in his retreat, in the safety which it offers, is now firing at us, not knowing that we would like nothing better than to come to his aid against the real enemy.' We should also mention another statement from Codreanu in answer to our question about his attitude towards the King: 'Well, we are all monarchists; it is just that we cannot renounce our mission and strike compromises with an outdated and corrupt world.'

Codreanu offered to take us back to our hotel in his own car, with no concern for the sensation this might have stirred. Nor, on our part, did we heed the warning given by our legation, which had told us that anyone who met with Codreanu would be expelled from the Kingdom within twenty-four hours. Taking his leave from us, knowing that we were headed for Berlin and Rome, Codreanu told us, 'Send my regards to all those who are fighting for our cause and let them know that Romanian Legionarism is and will be unconditionally on their side in the anti-Jewish, anti-democratic and anti-Bolshevik struggle.'

As had already been intimated to us in Bucharest, an Italian translation of Codreanu's book, entitled *The Iron Guard*, has recently been published as part of the *Europa Giovane* series (Casa Editrice Nazionale, Roma-Torino, 1938). This is the first part of a work which simultaneously serves as Codreanu's autobiography and as a history of his

struggle and of his movement, interwoven of course with an expo-
sition of his doctrine and of his nationalist programme. This book
may be fruitfully compared to the first part of *Mein Kampf* without
the risk of it losing any of its value through the comparison. Indeed,
it is the very power, or even tragedy of things which contributes to
make Codreanu's narrative particularly suggestive. Through it, we
believe that all Fascists may become aware of the tragic and painful
vicissitudes of a struggle which, on Romanian soil, has mirrored the
struggle of our own anti-democratic and anti-Jewish revolutions. It
is high time for the truth to be known about such things, for so far it
has been concealed or distorted by a biased press. Nor is it possible
to get a clear idea of what changes may be in store for Romania in the
future if one ignores the Legionary movement, which, while suffering
repression, is certainly far from extinct.

Because of its very nature, Codreanu's book is difficult to sum
up. Here, we shall only mention some of its general and doctrinal
points, in order to help define the character of Codreanu's movement. Already in 1919 or 1920, just over the age of twenty, Codreanu
rose up against the Communist peril in the name of the Romanian
nation, not so much with words as with action worthy of a *squadrista*,
fighting workers in revolt and replacing the red flags they had raised
in their factories with national ones. A follower of A. C. Cuza, the
father of Romanian nationalism and a forerunner of the anti-Semitic
struggle, Codreanu by that time had already learned what the victory of Communism would really have entailed: not a Romania led
by a proletarian Romanian regime, but rather the enslavement of the
country, right from day two of the revolution, to 'the dirtiest tyranny:
the Talmudic, Jewish tyranny'.[1] Israel, however, never forgives those
who unmask its plans. Already at that time, Codreanu was made into
the *bête noire* of the press sponsored by Israel and the object of a sav-
age smear and hate campaign – one launched not only against him,
but against the national faith of an entire people. More or less in this
period, Codreanu wrote, 'I learned enough anti-Semitism in one year
to last me three lifetimes. For one cannot strike the sacred beliefs of a
people or what their heart loves and respects, without hurting them to
the depths and without blood dripping from their wound. Seventeen
years have passed since and the wound is still bleeding.' Codreanu
was then fighting against those singing the praises of the Red International. His followers smashed the printing houses of Jewish rags
which insulted the King, the army, and the Church. Later, however, it

---

1   All quotes from *The Iron Guard* in this essay are taken from the English transla-
    tion, *For My Legionaries* (Reedy, West Virginia: Liberty Bell Publications, 2003).

was precisely in the name of the King, of the army, and of order that a Romanian press, with an expert's skill in jumping on the bandwagon, was to resume the same campaign against Codreanu himself, piling hatred and contempt upon his movement...

Codreanu writes:

> I could not describe how I entered this fight. Perhaps as a man who, walking down the street with his worries and thoughts, is surprised by the fire which consumes a house, takes off his coat, jumping to the aid of those engulfed by flames. I, with the mind of a youth of 19-20 years of age, understood from all that I saw that we were losing our country, that we were no longer going to have a country, that by the unconscious collaboration of the poor Romanian workingmen, impoverished and exploited, the ruling and devastating Jewish horde would engulf us. I acted on orders from my heart, from an instinct of defence possessed by even the least crawling worm, not out of an instinct for mere personal preservation, but one for defending the people of whom I was a part. That is why, all the time, I had the feeling that the whole people was behind us, with all the living, with all those who have died for their country, with its future generations; that our people fights and speaks through us, that the enemy numbers, no matter how large, faced with this historic entity, are but a handful of human wretches that we will scatter and vanquish. ...
>
> The individual within the framework and in the service of his people. The people within the framework and in the service of their God and of God's laws. Whoever shall understand these things will be victorious even if he be alone. Whoever shall not understand will be defeated.

This was Codreanu's profession of faith in 1922, at the end of his studies at university. As President of the Nationalist Association of law students, he summed up the main points of the anti-Semitic campaign as follows:

> a) The identification, at every step, of this Judaic spirit and mentality, that has stealthily infiltrated the thinking and feeling pattern of a large portion of Romanians.
>
> b) Our detoxification: namely, the elimination of Judaism that was introduced into our thinking through books in schools,

literature, and professors, as well as through lectures, theatre and cinematography.

c) The understanding and the unmasking of the Jewish plans hidden behind so many forms. For we have political parties, led by Romanians, through which Judaism speaks; Romanian newspapers that are written by Romanians, through which the Jew speaks for his interests; Romanian lecturers and authors, thinking, writing and speaking Hebrew in the Romanian language.

Codreanu simultaneously engaged with practical problems of a political, national and social nature, namely: the problem of vast tracts of Romanian land literally colonised by an exclusively Jewish population; the problem of Jewish control of vital centres in larger cities; the problem of the alarming percentage of Jews in schools, to the point where they often constitute an overwhelming majority – a percentage amounting to a preparation for a takeover and an invasion of the professional field open to the new generation. Finally, a simple action of unmasking: just as in the Communist period, Codreanu had revealed that the leaders of the so-called Romanian proletarian movement were all Jews, so later, as a member of Parliament, he did not hesitate to prove that most members of the government were receiving 'money loans' from Jewish banks.

At the advent of Mussolini, Codreanu acknowledged him as a 'bright North Star giving us hope; he will be living proof that the hydra can be defeated; proof of the possibilities of victory'. He added, '"But Mussolini is not anti-Semitic. You rejoice in vain", whispered the Jewish press into our ears. It is not a matter of what we rejoice in say I, it is a question of why you Jews are sad at his victory, if he is not anti-Semitic. What is the rationale of the worldwide attack on him by the Jewish press?' Codreanu rightly saw that Judaism has managed to dominate the world through Freemasonry and Russia through Communism. 'Judaism has become master of the world through Masonry, and in Russia through Communism. Mussolini destroyed at home these two Judaic heads which threatened death to Italy: Communism and Masonry', Codreanu argues. 'There, Judaism was eradicated through its two manifestations.' The new anti-Semitic turn of Fascism has proven Codreanu completely right.

In order to bring Codreanu's anti-Semitic outlook fully to light, it is worth quoting the following passage from his book in its entirety, for its vision is a particularly clear one:

Whoever imagines that the Jews are some poor unfortunates who arrived here haphazardly, brought by winds, pushed by fate, etc., is mistaken. All Jews over the entire world form a great collectivity bound together by blood and by the Talmudic religion. They are constituted into a very strict state, having laws, plans, and leaders making these plans. At the foundation, there is the Kehilla.[2] So, we do not face some isolated Jews but a constituted power, the Jewish community. In every city or market town where a number of Jews settle, the Kehilla, the Jewish community there is immediately formed. This Kehilla has its own leaders, separate judicial set-up, taxes, etc., and holds the entire Jewish population of that locality tightly united around itself. It is here, in this tiny Kehilla of a market town or city, that all plans are made: how to win over local politicians and authorities; how to infiltrate certain circles of interest to them, such as magistrates, officers, and high officials; what plans to use to take over such and such branch of commerce from the hands of a Romanian; how to destroy a local anti-Semite; how to destroy an incorruptible representative of local authority who might oppose Jewish interests; what plans to apply when, squeezed beyond endurance, the populace would revolt and erupt into anti-Semitic movements.

Besides this are far-reaching general plans:

1. They will try to break the spiritual ties of the Romanian to heaven, and to earth. To break our ties with heaven they will engage in widespread dissemination of atheistic theories in order to separate the Romanian people or at least some of the leaders from God; separating them from God and their dead they can destroy them, not by sword but by severing the roots of their spiritual life. To break our ties binding us to the land, the material source of a nation's existence, they will attack nationalism, labeling it 'outmoded', and everything related to the idea of fatherland and soil, in order to cut the thread of love tying the Romanian people to their furrow.

2. In order to succeed in this, they will endeavour to get control of the press.

---

2   Kehillas were local Jewish community leadership councils that existed throughout central and eastern Europe during the first half of the Twentieth century.

3. They will take advantage of every opportunity to sow discord in the Romanian camp, spreading misunderstandings, quarrels, and if possible to split it into factions fighting each other.

4. They will seek to gain control of most of the means of livelihood of the Romanians.

5. They will systematically urge Romanians on to licentiousness, destroying their families and their moral fiber.

6. They will poison and daze them with all kinds of drinks and other poisons. Anyone wishing to conquer and destroy a people could do it by using this system.

From the immediate aftermath of the War down to the most recent past, in all sectors and by all available means, Codreanu's movement has sought to counter the Jewish offensive launched in Romania by the two and a half million Israelites present on its soil and by the forces affiliated to or financed by Israel.

The plague of political schemers and the necessity of creating a 'new man' are other central points in Codreanu's thought. This kind of man who is alive today in Romanian politics we earlier met in history', Codreanu wrote. 'Nations died under his rule and states collapsed.' According to Codreanu, the greatest national peril lies in the fact that the pure type of the Dacio-Romanian race has been deformed and disfigured and has been replaced by the 'political schemer' – this 'moral freak who no longer possesses any trace of the nobleness of our race, and who is dishonouring and killing us'. As long as political schemers exist, hidden anti-national forces will always find suitable tools and will always be able to weave intrigues to serve their plot. While the Romanian Constitution of 1938 has put an end to the party system, many years ago Codreanu already had developed an approach to the matter so radical as to claim that, 'No youth must ever enter the gate of a political party; he who does so is a traitor to his generation and his nation.'

It is not a matter of new parties or formulae, but of creating a new man. It is this view that gave rise to Codreanu's Legion, which is primarily a school of life for the forging of a new type displaying 'all the possibilities of human grandeur that are implanted by God in the blood of our people'. The first Legionary organisation was called 'The Legion of Michael the Archangel'. Its very name points to the mystical, religious and ascetic aspects of its nationalism. The creation of this new type of man is the essential thing, according to Codreanu; the rest is only of secondary importance and will follow as an inevitable consequence in a natural and irresistible process. Through this regenerated man, the Jewish problem will be solved and a new political order will be established, awakening the kind of magnetism that is capable of carrying crowds away, of bringing victory, and of leading the race along the path of glory.

A particular and distinguishing aspect of the Romanian Legionary movement is the fact that, through its very structuring in 'nests', it was chiefly concerned with establishing a new form of shared living, based on strict ethical and religious criteria. It may come as a surprise to discover that Codreanu had imposed the discipline of the fast two days a week, and it is also interesting to note his thoughts on the power of prayer, thoughts which sound more like those of a religious than a political leader:

> Prayer is a decisive element for victory. ... Wars were won by those who knew how to summon the mysterious powers of the unseen world from above and to ensure their help. These mysterious powers are the souls of the dead, the souls of our ancestors who too were once attached to this land, to our furrows, and who died in the defense of this land, and who today also are attached to it by the memory of their life here, and through us - their children, grand-children and great-great-grandchildren. But above all the souls of the dead stands God.
>
> When these powers are summoned, they come to our aid and encourage us, to give us strength of will and everything necessary to help us to achieve victory. They introduce panic and terror into the hearts of the enemy and paralyse their actions. In the last analysis, victory does not depend on material preparation or on the material strength of the belligerents, but on their capacity to ensure the support of the spiritual powers. ...
>
> By the justness and morality of your actions, and by appealing fervently and insistently to these powers, invoke them, attract them by the strength of your soul and they will come. The power of attraction is the greater when the appeal, the prayer, is made by many people assembled together.

Here is another characteristic passage by Codreanu:

If Christian mysticism aiming at ecstasy is man's contact with God, through a 'jump from human nature into the divine one' (Crainic), national mysticism is nothing more than man's contact, or that of the multitude, with the soul of their people, through a jump outside of personal preoccupations into the eternal life of the people. Not intellectually, for this could be done by any historian, but living, with their soul.

Another typical aspect of the Legionarism of the 'Iron Guard' is a sort of ascetic commitment on the part of their leaders: they must refrain from going to dance halls, cinemas or theatres and must avoid any display of wealth or even mere affluence. A special assault corps of 10,000 men, named after Mota and Marin (the two leaders of the 'Iron Guards' who fell in Spain), like one of the ancient knightly orders, enforced the rule of celibacy upon its members for as long as they remained in the corps, for no mundane or family occupation was to diminish their readiness to embrace death at any moment.

While Codreanu twice served as a member of Parliament, right from the start he took a firm stance against democracy. To quote him verbatim, democracy breaks the unity of the race through party factionalism; it is incapable of continuity in terms of effort and responsibility; it is incapable of displaying authority, since it lacks the power of sanction and turns the politician into the slave of his partisans; it serves the interests of big finance; and finally, it makes millions of Jews Romanian citizens. In contrast, Codreanu asserted the principle of social selection and of elites. He clearly foresaw the new politics of nations striving for reconstruction, whose underlying principle is neither democracy nor dictatorship, but rather the relationship between nation and leader – potency and act, obscure instinct and expression. The leader of these new forms of government is not elected by the crowd; rather, the crowd, or nation, lends its consent to him and recognises its own ideas in his

The premise here is a sort of inner awakening, starting from the leader and the elites. It is worth quoting Codreanu's words:

Without defining them one must admit that they represent a new form of government, *sui generis*, in the modern states. It has not been encountered up to now and I do not know what name it will be given.

I believe that it has at its basis that state of spirit, that state of elevated national conscience which, sooner or later, spreads to the outskirts of the national organism.

It is a state of inner revelation. That which of old was the people's instinctive repository is reflected in these moments in the people's conscience, creating a state of unanimous illumination which is encountered only in the great religious revivals. This phenomenon could rightly be called a state of national ecumenicity. A people in its entirety reaches an awareness of self, of its purpose and destiny in the world. During past history only flashes of such awareness have been noticed, but today we are faced with some permanent such phenomena.

In such a case the leader is no longer a 'master', a 'dictator', who does as he 'pleases', who leads 'according to his whims'. He is the incarnation of this unseen state of spirit, the symbol of this state of consciousness. He no longer does 'as he pleases', he does what he 'must' do. And he is guided not by individual or collective interests, but by the interests of the immortal nation which have penetrated the conscience of the people. It is only within the framework of these interests and only in that framework that personal and collective interests find their maximum of normal satisfaction.

Codreanu never ruled out that these new forms of nationalism could be combined with traditional institutions, as is proven by his ideas on the monarchical institution, conveyed through the following words:

At the head of peóples, above the elite, one finds the monarchy. I reject the republic. …Not all of the monarchs were good. Monarchy itself, however, has always been good. One must not confuse the man with the institution and draw false conclusions. There can be bad priests; but can we, because of this, conclude that the Church must be abolished and God stoned to death? There are weak and bad monarchs, certainly, but we cannot renounce monarchy because of this. …

To each nation God has traced a line of destiny. A monarch is great and good when he stays on that line; he is small or bad, to the extent that he wanders away from this line of destiny or opposes it. This then, is the law of monarchy. There are also other lines that may tempt a monarch: the line of personal interest or that of a class of people or group; the line of alien interests (domestic or foreign). He must avoid all these lines and follow that of his people.

While in the main these are the ideas of Codreanu and his 'Iron Guard', the vicissitudes of his struggle appear tragically incomprehensible; until just recently, they appeared merely to be the result of some wretched misunderstanding. Until recently, that is, because for as long as a purely democratic regime existed in Romania, one known to be subject to all sorts of indirect and masked influences, with the monarchy having a simply symbolic function, it was understandable for a movement such as Codreanu's to be hampered by all means and at any cost – one day by one formula, the next by the opposite one, according to expediency, provided the same effect was achieved and the dangerous enemy undermined. It was easy to understand then the following bitter observations made by Codreanu:

> In 1919, 1920, 1921, the entire Jewish press was assaulting the Romanian state, unleashing disorder everywhere, urging violence against the regime, the form of government, the church, Romanian order, the national idea, patriotism.
>
> Now, as if by a miracle, the same press, controlled by the same men, changed into a defender of the state's order, of laws; declares itself against violence. While we become: 'the country's enemies', 'extremists of the Right', 'in the pay and service of Romania's enemies', etc. And in the end we will hear also this: that we are financed by the Jews. …
>
> We have endured outrage after outrage, ridicule after ridicule, slap after slap, until we have come to see ourselves in this frightening situation: Jews are considered to be defenders of Romanianism, sheltered from any unpleasantness, leading a life of peace and plenty, while we are considered enemies of our nation, with our liberty and life endangered, and we are hunted down like rabid dogs by all the Romanian authorities.
>
> I witnessed with my own eyes these times and lived through them, and I was saddened to the depths of my soul. It is dreadful to fight for years on end for your fatherland, your heart as pure as tears, while enduring misery and hunger, then find yourself suddenly declared an enemy of your country, persecuted by your own kind, told that you fight because you are in the pay of foreigners, and see the entire Jewry master your land, assuming the role of defender of Romanianism and caretaker of the Romanian state, menaced by you, the youth of the country. Night after night we were troubled by these thoughts, occasionally feeling disgusted and immensely ashamed and we were seized by sadness.

The reader will soon realise that these are not mere words by going through Codreanu's book, which documents the entire *via crucis* of the 'Iron Guard' – all the arrests, persecutions, trials, defamation, and violence. Codreanu himself had undergone several trials, but until just recently he had always been acquitted. This was also the case when he was tried for murder for having killed his comrades' executioners with his own hands; and it is indeed remarkable that on this occasion 19,300 lawyers from all over the country officially offered to defend him.

After the Goga experiment, the democratic regime seemed to have come to an end in Romania and to have been replaced by a new, authoritarian form of government. Few of the details behind these upheavals are known abroad. Although the 'Iron Guard' had already been disbanded, in this new phase of Romanian politics, the struggle nevertheless continued between Codreanu and the forces opposed to his conception of the nation and state. The Goga government was supposedly set up both as an experiment and for a precise tactical purpose. By means of Goga's moderate nationalism and anti-Semitism, an attempt was made to sidetrack the forces which Codreanu's movement was increasingly winning over to his side, by offering a substitute easy to tame. However, to quote the expression Mussolini used for the plebiscite proclaimed by Schuschnigg,[3] it was soon realised that the experiment was a dangerous one and that the device could go off any minute in the hands of those who had assembled it. People did not regard Goga's as an ersatz regime with which to be content, but rather as a sign of preliminary assent to the revolutionary nationalist current. Little did it matter that Goga resolutely opposed Codreanu (and this was indeed one of the reasons why he was chosen in the first place); what mattered was rather his programme, which inclined towards nationalism and anti-Semitism – as well as a re-thinking of Romania's place in international politics. Hence, had the elections announced by Goga taken place, it is most likely that he would have been swept away by a current stronger than him, albeit one flowing in the same direction.

---

3   Kurt Schuschnigg was the Chancellor of Austria just prior to the *Anschluss* of March 1938. In response to a growing desire by Austrians for a unification with Germany, Schuschnigg called for a national plebiscite in February 1938 to vote on the issue of Austrian independence, but its terms were manipulated in such a way as to make a vote in favour of unification unlikely. Ultimately, the plebiscite was cancelled, Schuschnigg resigned, and Austria was annexed by Germany.

Acknowledging this threat, the King decided to personally intervene. He put an end to the democratic party system and had a Constitution promulgated, the central feature of which was the centralisation of power directly or indirectly in the hands of the monarch. This has been described as an authoritarian revolution from above, initiated from within the court instead of the public square. In the face of this, the 'Iron Guard' moved ahead of its enemy and spontaneously disbanded the party it had founded, 'All for the Fatherland'. It then silently withdrew with the aim of essentially focusing its action on the spiritual level, in such a way as to spiritually shape and select the vast number of followers who in this latter period – particularly in view of what was expected to follow Goga's government – had flocked to join Codreanu's ranks.

We were in Romania at the time, and the solution which the most serious Romanians considered desirable and likely was the overcoming of the former opposition between the regime and Legionarism, and a collaboration between the two on a national basis. This opinion was not only held by the chief Romanian theoretician of the state, Manoilescu, and by those, such as Nae Jonescu, who had significantly aided the return of the King to his fatherland; the minister Argetoianu himself, the main inspiration for the new Constitution, in a conversation we had with him at the time, did not rule out the possibility of cooperation of this kind, provided – as he put it – that the 'Iron Guard' renounced its former methods.

Clearly, we do not wish to deny that under normal conditions, with its power and significance intact, monarchy requires no dictatorial surrogate in order to properly perform its function. This is not the case, however, in a state where traditional *fides*[4] has been replaced by political intrigue, in which the Jewish hydra has wrapped its tentacles around the chief vital cores of the nation, and in which electoral democracy has undermined the ethical integrity and patriotic feelings of large sectors of the political world. These conditions call for a totalitarian movement of renewal, something which, through a collective drive, will prove capable of overwhelming, re-founding, transforming and elevating the whole nation, essentially on the basis of a new state of consciousness and the power of an ideal and faith. If present, the institution of the monarchy will not be brought down by a totalitarian national movement of this sort; rather, it will find strength and completeness in it, as the very example of Italy goes to show. In these terms, a collaboration between the new regime and Codreanu's national Legionary movement was deemed both desirable

---

4   Loyalty.

and possible, particularly since, as we have seen, Codreanu expressly defended the idea of monarchy and never planned to offer himself as the new King of Romania – something which even his opponents have never implied.

The most recent events have shown these hopes to be illusory by precipitating the tragedy. Not long after the final approval of the new Constitution, Codreanu was once again arrested. Why? At first, because many months after the incident it was suddenly recalled that he had once insulted a minister – something that, throughout his career, under the pressure of circumstance, he had in fact never been able to avoid doing. Later he was accused of plotting against the security of the state. The truth is that Codreanu's arrest took place almost the day after the *Anschluss*. Therefore, it was most probably due to a fear that the National Socialist triumph in Austria might unleash the forces of Romanian nationalism held at bay until then. The leader of these forces had to be eliminated one way or the other. The trial ended with a ten-year prison sentence for Codreanu. At the same time, a group of sub-leaders was arrested, along with a number of people suspected of being members or sympathisers of the 'Guard'. It became clear that the situation was getting worse and that the national political situation in Romania was far from acquiring stability. It is also evident that while the previous trials against Codreanu had invariably ended with his acquittal – despite the fact that democratic corruption at the time was making things easy for the forces opposing him – he was instead pronounced guilty under the new anti-democratic and 'national' Constitution. This sentence effectively amounted to an open challenging of all the forces of national Romanian Legionarism, still as present and numerous as ever, if perhaps concealed and no longer easy to identify. And although few details are known of this new trial, it is clear that the sentence was either too severe or not severe enough: for if Codreanu could really have positively been convicted of plotting against the state, given the animus which had led to the trial, this would have been the finest opportunity to get rid of him once and for all, since the new Constitution punished this crime with the death penalty. Instead, Codreanu was only given ten years.

What they did not dare to do at that time, however, they did later on; and what could then be foreseen inevitably happened. After an initial moment of bewilderment, the forces loyal to Codreanu embarked upon a terrorist course of retaliation. The 'death battalion' went into action and a secret 'national tribunal' was set up to pass judgement upon and smite those considered to be the most guilty towards the nation from a Legionary perspective. This upheaval acquired momentum following the capitulation of Prague and the Munich Pact, but unfortunately it only led to an increasingly difficult situation: more and more people were arrested and one act of injustice led to another. Recently, there has been the assassination of the Rector of Cluj University, who was particularly hostile to the 'Guard'; two provincial governors have been sentenced to the death penalty – to be carried out by January – by the secret Legionary 'national tribunal'; and such a feeling of insecurity was in the air that high-ranking personalities, including a prince of royal blood and General Antonescu – the former War Minister of the Goga government and current commander of the Second Army Corps – have been removed, banned or arrested. Things have intensified with the two sides becoming increasingly embittered, and we have reached the final stage of the tragedy. On the 30th of November, a laconic official communiqué announced that Codreanu, together with thirty other Legionaries – leading cadres of the movement who had also been arrested – was killed by the police after trying to escape. Their corpses were apparently buried three hours later – that is, almost immediately – thus preventing any further investigation.

We have now reached the breaking point. The impression made by Codreanu's death throughout Romania, where his supporters numbered in the millions, is huge, and the state of siege which was already in force in various regions has been extended to the whole Kingdom. The situation in Romania appears as murky as it has been only in rare moments of its history.

We have seen and noted that either we are to believe that Codreanu was completely in bad faith – something which can easily be ruled out by anyone who ever met him, even just for a few minutes, or who has perceived the faith, enthusiasm and deep sincerity suffusing each of his writings; or we cannot concede that his movement was in any way subversive or that it pursued aims other than those of a national and anti-Semitic reconstruction of the 'Fascist' or National Socialist type, respectful of the monarchic principle. What, then? We may legitimately wonder about the real forces which have caused, or at least contributed to the tragedy of the 'Iron Guard'. At the time of Codreanu's last arrest, we were in Paris and witnessed the shouts of frenzied joy that accompanied the publication of this news in antifascist and Judeo-socialist rags. We are not going too far if we say that, after Czechoslovakia, in the whole of central-eastern Europe, Romania is the last strategically and economically important area with a wealth of resources to remain outside the web woven by the obscure 'forces' at work in the 'great democracies', in high finance, and in

Judeo-socialism. For such forces it is a mere trifle to favour the interests of short-sighted individuals as a means and an end while treading upon people's corpses, even the corpses of noble and generous youths whose only concern was with the good of their country...

(Originally printed in La Vita Italiana, *Rome, issue 309, December 1938.)*

VI
MY MEETING WITH CODREANU

I have met several exponents of the movements for national reconstruction which surfaced in the period between the two World Wars,
and I remember Corneliu Codreanu, the leader of the Romanian Iron
Guard, as being one of the purest, noblest and most righteous among
these men. Our meeting took place in the spring of 1938, when I was
visiting Bucharest in one of the journeys I was then undertaking to
explore various European countries.

Corneliu Codreanu's very physical appearance was striking. Tall
and well-proportioned, he embodied the 'Aryo-Roman' racial type,
which is also to be found in Romania, no doubt on account both of the
Roman colonisation of Dacia and of the Indo-European stock of the
pre-existing local population. Codreanu's appearance and his manner
of speech gave one the unmistakable impression that he was a man
who knew no deviousness, insincerity, disloyalty, or treachery. This
greatly contributed to the unique authority he enjoyed amongst his
followers, who were bound to him by ties far deeper and more personal than those of mere politics.

There was much tension in Romania at the time between the
King's government and the Iron Guard. The climate that was to have
such tragic consequences was then in the making. I had been told by
the Italian embassy that it was not safe to approach Codreanu, for the
Romanian authorities had already proceeded to immediately expel
strangers who had met him. But I did not heed this warning. A Romanian I was already in contact with – for he was someone interested in
traditional studies – acted as a go-between.

Not long after I had voiced my desire to see Codreanu, two envoys
of his made a silent appearance in my hotel room, offering to take
me to meet their leader in the so-called 'Green House'. Built by the

Legionaries themselves in the outskirts of Bucharest, this building served as the movement's headquarters.

After what appears to be a traditional Romanian rite of hospitality – I was served a small plate with a sort of jam, and a glass of water – Codreanu introduced himself. A feeling of mutual sympathy immediately arose between the two of us. Codreanu was familiar with my book, *Revolt Against the Modern World*, which two years earlier had also been published in a German translation, arousing much interest in central Europe. My concern for the need to give political struggle a spiritual and traditional foundation is what helped foster our mutual understanding. As I do not know Romanian, Codreanu spoke to me in French, and did so in a rather hesitant manner that enabled him to express his thoughts with careful precision and conciseness.

Among the various arguments of our conversation, I recall the interesting way in which Codreanu defined Fascism, German National Socialism, and his own movement. He argued that there are three aspects to each organism: form, vital force, and the spirit. The same is true of nations and so each renovation movement will develop by stressing a particular one of these principles. According to Codreanu, what prevailed in Fascism was form, in the sense of that informing power that shapes states and civilisations – something reflecting the heritage of Rome as an organising power. National Socialism instead emphasised vital force most of all, hence the importance it assigned to race and the myth of race, and its appeal to the idea of blood and of national-racial community. The Iron Guard's starting point was instead believed to be the spiritual element. This is where Codreanu wished to begin. And what he meant by 'spirit' was something also connected to strictly religious and ascetic values.

Codreanu claimed that there was something wrong with the Romanian people. The essential premise for him was the need for profound renovation, which was to begin from within individuals and then be directed chiefly against all that which is subject to mere desire for profit, lowly interests, political scheming, and urban economic speculation. What Codreanu was interested in, therefore, was creating a movement, not a party; and he hardly trusted the attempt that was then being made to consolidate the country through a democratic superstructure, albeit one controlled by the monarchy. When we were discussing the question of religion, Codreanu mentioned the fact that he regarded the historical situation Romania found itself in as a favourable one, as in Orthodox Christianity there was no opposition between the universalism of faith and the idea of the nation: as a national Church, the Orthodox one could serve as an allied counterpart to a state renewed by national revolution.

Religious and, often, even mystical and ascetic values thus served as a foundation for the Romanian Iron Guard movement. One of its embodiments bore the name 'Legion of St. Michael the Archangel'. Not only prayer but fasting, too, was practised. The leaders of the movement were to lead an austere life, without ever attending public entertainment events, theatres, and profane celebrations. They were never to display any luxury and wealth. Marriage itself was discouraged, as they had to devote their own persons to the fullest extent.

The Legion was also marked by a certain mystique of death. The rite of 'Present!', also known to Fascism, was practised in such a way that some people have regarded it as a kind of magical evocation. Mota and Marin, two Romanian Legionaries who had been friends of Codreanu's and had fallen in the Spanish war, were the objects of a sort of worship.

In the course of our long conversation, Codreanu discussed many other matters. He then personally drove me back to my hotel, almost as a challenge – I have already mentioned the warning I had been given by the Italian embassy. When I asked him whether the Iron Guard had any badge, Codreanu gave me one. This consisted of a small circle not unlike that which the SS used to wear when in civilian dress. It featured a sort of grey grid set against a black background. When I asked Codreanu the meaning of this pattern, he jokingly replied, 'It might be prison bars.'

Unfortunately, this joke contained a sad premonition. We all know what fate awaited Codreanu. The King, in the thralls of the Jewess Lupescu[1] and of her female charms, along with his 'democratic' government, comprised of men loyal to Freemasonry and other dark forces, chose the shortest path to get rid of the Iron Guard, which was then increasingly attracting the healthy strata of the Romanian population. Mass arrests took place, and Codreanu himself was arrested. He was suppressed just like Ettore Muti[2] was: they claimed that he

---

1   Magda Lupescu was an ethnic Jew who was raised as a Catholic. She became the mistress to King Carol II in the 1920s and he even abdicated the throne to maintain his relationship with her, although circumstances permitted his later return. By many accounts she was a crude woman who enjoyed flaunting her status. They were later married after his second abdication.

2   Muti was a prominent Italian Fascist who was arrested shortly after the coup against Mussolini in July 1943, and subsequently shot by the police, who claimed he had been trying to escape. The circumstances around this killing have always been regarded as suspicious.

was shot as he was trying to escape. The King, however, only hastened his own demise. General Antonescu, a former follower of Codreanu, came into power. Eventually Romania, too, was overwhelmed by the military collapse of the Axis, and the Red Army imposed the current Communist regime upon the country.

Still, quite a few members of the Iron Guard survive. Now living in exile, they remain loyal to their leader's ideal and are active in several nationalist groups in Belgium, Switzerland, and especially Spain – as well as France. In this country they were amongst those who helped develop an at least partly spiritual and traditional ideology for the military movement that was later betrayed and suppressed by de Gaulle. After this event, they joined the OAS or similar organisations.[3] Codreanu's legacy, then, continues to live on.

(Originally printed in Civiltà, *Rome, no. 2, September-October 1973.)*

---

3   Evola is referring to the May 1958 crisis, when a Right-wing coup seized control of the Algerian colonial government and threatened a similar action in France if de Gaulle was not made President. Although de Gaulle gained power as a result of this coup, he later betrayed his former comrades, who had formed the Right-wing OAS with the intention of preserving Algeria as a French colony, by allowing Algerian independence.

APPENDIX 2:

PHOTOGRAPHS OF CODREANU
AND THE IRON GUARD

Codreanu and fellow students during the trial of 1923. Codreanu and his comrades were nicknamed 'Vacaresteni' after the Vacaresti prison where they were incarcerated.

Corneliu Codreanu and his wife Elena. The picture was taken in the village Pinet-d'Uriage near Grenoble, during Codreanu's studies in France, 1925-1927.

Corneliu Codreanu and his wife Elena Codreanu (née Ilinoiu) on their wedding day. The marriage ceremony took place on 13 June 1925 and was attended by 100,000 people.

The small house in the middle of the picture is where the Codreanus lived during their stay in Pinet-d'Uriage.

Corneliu Codreanu and his wife Elena with the Belmain family wintering in Pinet-d'Uriage.

Codreanu with a group of Legionaries in 1932 or 1933. The man to the right is Mihai Stelescu.

The Italian Fascist politician Eugenio Coselschi visiting Codreanu at the Green House in October 1934.

Using a horn, Codreanu signals that it is time to stop working.

Codreanu at the Legionary work camp Carmen Sylva in 1935.

Codreanu climbs the mountain Raraului, accompanied by Constantin Papanace.

Ion Mota and Codreanu saluting Hristache Solomon's coffin.

General Cantacuzino-Grănicerul inspects works.

Codreanu explaining the work programme to a group of labourers.

Professor Dobre teaches Codreanu to shoot with a bow and arrow.

Codreanu supervising work.

Codreanu with visitors at Camp Carmen Sylva.

Codreanu at Camp Hotarele.

The peak Pietrele Doamnei in the Rarau mountains – Codreanu's favourite spot for meditation.

Codreanu at work in the Legionary Movement's brickyard at Giulesti, near Bucharest.

Codreanu at work at the headquarters on Gutenberg street, Bucharest.

A group of Legionaries who fought in the Spanish Civil War.

Codreanu and Vasile Iasinschi at the Cernauti train station.

Train carrying the bodies of dead comrades at the train station at Roman.

Train carrying martyred Legionaries rolls into the train station at Bacau, 9 February 1937.

Codreanu and the Spanish ambassador Prat y Soutzo attend a ceremony in Bucharest.

Codreanu and the Spanish ambassador Prat y Soutzo at the North train station in Bucharest.

Codreanu and General
Cantacuzino-Grănicerul.

General Cantacuzino-Grănicerul, Codreanu and the Spanish ambassador
Prat y Soutzo on the steps of the St. Ilie Gorgani church in Bucharest, after
a religious service.

Legionary funeral procession.

Codreanu with Legionary veterans of the war in Spain.

The mausoleum of Ion Mota and Vasile Marin at the Green House.

Codreanu at General Cantacuzino-Grănicerul's funeral.

The funeral of General Cantacuzino-Grănicerul, 11 November 1937.

Crowd in the street in front of the Green House.

Codreanu at the head of a column of Legionaries.

Photograph of Codreanu, published in the French magazine Le Mois *in 1938.*

Codreanu and the leader of the party Totul Pentru Tara, the engineer Gheorghe Clime.

Codreanu and General Antonescu skiing in Predeal.

Codreanu at an inauguration ceremony. The man to the right of him is Colonel Zavoianu.

Codreanu in 1938.

A photograph of the so-called Decemvirii, the group of students and workers who killed Mihai Stelescu.

Miti Dumitrescu, one of the nine Legionaries who avenged Codreanu by killing Armand Calinescu, the man responsible for the murder of Codreanu and hundreds of Legionaries. Dumitrescu and his men became known as the Razbunatorii, i.e., the 'Avengers'.

Following the killing of Armand Calinescu, Miti Dumitrescu and his men turned themselves in to the authorities, declaring that they had executed Calinescu as punishment for Codreanu's murder. They were tortured and put to death by the police, without trial. The picture shows the bodies of the Razbunatorii lying in the street.

The car in which Armand Calinescu travelled when he was gunned down by Miti Dumitrescu and his team of Legionaries.

Codreanu's funeral.

Procession at Codreanu's funeral.

Books published by Logik Förlag

Berlin, Saga, Jacobson, Mats, (2013). *Djuren i Yggdrasil.*
Björkqvist, Björn, red., (2005). *En annan bild av Hitler.*
Björkqvist, Björn, (2014). *Vägvalet.*
Burnham, Stanley, (2015). *Svart intelligens i ett vitt samhälle.*
Carlberg, Carl-Ernfrid, (2012). *Texter, dikter och bilder.*
Chamberlain, Houston Stewart, (2015). *Demokrati och frihet.*
Codreanu, Corneliu Z., (2007). *Till mina legionärer.*
Dahlberg, Per, (2006). *Den nordiska ledartanken.*
Degrelle, Léon, (2006). *Epos.*
Degrelle, Léon, (2012). *Fälttåget i Ryssland.*
Dixon Jr., Thomas, (2015). *Vita ryttare.*
Duke, David, (2015). *Den judiska rasismen.*
Duke, David, (2013). *Kämpa för nordisk frihet.*
Eckehart, Meister, (2007). *Hur Sverige blev en mångkultur.*
Faurisson, Robert, (2007). *Mitt liv som revisionist.*
Faurisson, Robert, (2008). *Revisionismens segrar.*
Flodæus, Olof, (2012). *Röd död.*
Garfvé, Henrik, (2006). *Ras och IQ.*
Hansson, Per, (2012). *Demokratin som dödgrävare.*
Harwood, Richard, (2008). *Nürnbergprocessen.*
Johnson, Greg, (2015) *Nya högern kontra Gamla högern.*
Kjellén, Rudolf, (2009). *Nationalitetsidén.*
Kjellman, Östen, (2013). *Tankar i skogen.*
Kjellman, Östen, (2013). *Vilka började andra världskriget?*
Lindholm, Sven Olov, (2012). *Svensk frihetskamp*
Macdonald, Andrew, (2012). *Jägaren.*
Macdonald, Andrew, (2009). *Turners dagböcker.*
MacDonald, Kevin, (2012). *Att förstå det judiska inflytandet.*
Nordengruppen, (2011). *Ett annat Tyskland.*
Rami, Ahmed, (2005). *Tabubelagda tankar.*
Rushton, J. Philippe (2014). *Ras, evolution och beteende.*
Söderman, Magnus, (2013). *Den trotsiga.*
Söderman, Magnus, (2011). *Till värn för Norden.*

CPSIA information can be obtained
at www.ICGtesting.com
Printed in the USA
BVHW080859090921
616322BV00007B/883